Web Pages in Microsoft C

Anna Callaghan

IT Key Skills

Other Titles of Interest

BP440	Explaining Microsoft Money 97
BP441	Creating Web Pages using Microsoft Office 97
BP442	Explaining Microsoft Publisher 97
BP452	A Practical Introduction to Microsoft Office 97
BP461	Using FrontPage 98
BP476	Microsoft PowerPoint 2000 Explained
BP477	Using Microsoft FrontPage 2000
BP480	A Practical Introduction to Sage Line 50
BP482	Sage Instant Accounting 2000

Web Pages using Microsoft Office 2000

David Weale

Bernard Babani (Publishing) Ltd
The Grampians
Shepherds Bush Road
London W6 7NF
England

Please Note

Although every care has been taken with the production of this book to ensure that any instructions or any of the other contents operate in a correct and safe manner, the Author and the Publishers do not accept any responsibility for any failure, damage or loss caused by following the said contents. The Author and Publisher do not take any responsibility for errors or omissions.

The Author and Publisher make no warranty or representation, either express or implied, with respect to the contents of this book, its quality, merchantability or fitness for a particular purpose.

The Author and Publisher will not be liable to the purchaser or to any other person or legal entity with respect to any liability, loss or damage (whether direct, indirect, special, incidental or consequential) caused or alleged to be caused directly or indirectly by this book.

The book is sold as is, without any warranty of any kind, either expressed or implied, respecting the contents, including but not limited to implied warranties regarding the book's quality, performance, correctness or fitness for any particular purpose.

No part of this book may be reproduced or copied by any means whatever without written permission of the publisher.

All rights reserved

© 2000 BERNARD BABANI (publishing) LTD

First Published - July 2000

British Library Cataloguing in Publication Data

A catalogue record for this book is available from the British Library

ISBN 0 85934 490 8

Cover Design by Gregor Arthur

Printed and bound in Great Britain by Guernsey Press

Preface

This book has provided me with many hours of pleasure. I hope you will experience the same delight in learning how to create and design your own web pages.

This book explains the use of Microsoft Word, Microsoft PowerPoint and Microsoft Publisher to create web pages, Access and Excel are also looked at briefly. There is an introduction to HTML, on-line forms, web design techniques and how to connect to the Internet and publish your pages.

The book will help you create web pages either for personal or business reasons, for use on the Internet or on an Intranet.

Best wishes,

David Weale May 2000

Trademarks

Microsoft®, MS-DOS, FrontPage®, PowerPoint®, and Windows® are registered trademarks or trademarks of Microsoft® Corporation.

All other trademarks are the registered and legally protected trademarks of the companies who make the products. There is no intent to use the trademarks generally and readers should investigate ownership of a trademark before using it for any purpose.

About the author

David Weale is a Fellow of the Institute of Chartered Accountants and has worked in both private and public practice. At present, he is a lecturer in business computing.

Contents

Common Features 1
Toolbars 2
Customising your toolbars 6
Insert hyperlink 6
Microsoft Office Programs 7

Word 2000 9
Word 10
Starting A New File 10
Web Page Wizard 11
Using a browser 19
Word files 22
Working with Word 25
Text 26
Working with graphics 30
Hyperlinks 34
Web Tools and Multi-media 36
Creating Forms 39
The Pull-down menus 40
File menu 40
Edit menu 41
View menu 41
Insert menu 41
Format menu 42
Tools menu 43
Table menu 44
Window menu 51
Help menu 51

MS Publisher 53
Wizards 54
The Step-through wizard questions 56
Publications by Design 68
Blank Publications 69
The pull-down menus 71
The File menu 71
Edit menu 73
View menu 74
Insert Menu 74
Format menu 79
Tools menu 79
Table menu 80
Help menu 80
PowerPoint 81
Saving the pages as HTML 82
Web file structure 85
Adding links & multi-media 86
Other Web Applications 91
Microsoft Applications 92
Excel 92
Access 93
Combinations 93
Publishing your Web 94

HTML Tutorial..95

Introduction to HTML 96
Fundamentals of HTML files...................................97
The main tags 98
Creating a file from scratch 100
Exercise one 101
Formatting tags.. 103
Exercise two 105
Ways of creating space(s).. 108
Exercise three 109
Exercise four.. 111
Background colours... 114
Exercise five 114
Adding graphics to your pages 115
Space and borders.. 116
Exercise six.. 117
Exercise seven 118
Exercise eight 119
Linking pages 122
Text links... 122
E-mail links 122
Exercise nine 123
Exercise ten 125
Lists 126
Exercise eleven... 129
Tables 131
Additional table tags.. 133
Exercise twelve.. 135

- Creating forms (using html)..137
  - Radio buttons...139
  - Checkboxes 141
  - Drop-Down menus 142
  - Text boxes 143
  - Submitting the form..144
- Frames..145
  - Setting up frames..145
  - Target frames..150

Other Considerations...155

- Designing web sites 156
  - First thoughts..156
  - General design tips 157
  - Backgrounds & fonts 159
  - Links..159
  - Text..160
  - Site Structure 162
  - Reverse engineering 162
  - Getting readers for your site 163
  - Will your pages be found?..164
  - What search engines index 165
  - How you access the Net 168
  - Connections 170
  - Domains...171
  - Hosting your web site...172

Glossary 173

Index..177

Common Features

Toolbars

The **Web** toolbar is common to all the applications.

If the toolbar does not appear automatically, then pull down the **View** menu, select **Toolbars** and then **Web**.

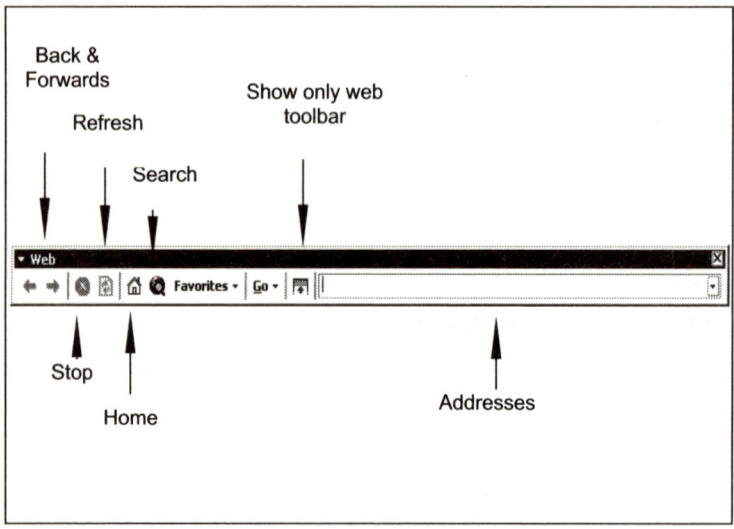

Back & Forward

These arrows move back to the previous web page you were looking at and (then) forward.

Stop

Stops the loading of the page you have selected, for example if it is taking too long or you made a mistake.

Refresh

This refreshes the page being shown (for example if changes have been made to the page).

Home/Start Page

Returns to your home or initial page.

Search the web

Connects you to the Internet.

Favorites

A list of sites you have found of particular interest and have added to your (own) list of favourite sites. You can add sites using this button, selecting **Add to Favorites**.

Go

Pulls down the menu shown below which replicates some of the buttons on the toolbar

Show only web toolbar

This hides the **standard** and **Formatting** toolbars.

Addresses

You can type in the address of a web site. In addition, clicking on the arrow to the right displays a list of addresses you have visited.

Web Tools toolbar

This toolbar is only available within certain applications e.g. Word.

Most of the buttons deal with the creation of on-line forms and are dealt with in that section, the last three deal with movies, sound and scrolling text and are dealt with in the multi-media section.

Customising your toolbars

The buttons on any toolbar can be altered to your own requirements.

If you want to add or remove individual buttons from your toolbars, pull down the **Tools** menu and select **Customise** followed by **Commands**.

Click and drag any commands onto the toolbar you want the button to appear on. Similarly remove any button by dragging it away from the toolbar.

Insert hyperlink

This button appears on the **Standard** toolbar. You use this button to insert a **hyperlink** (clickable text or image) that enables you to jump to another page on the Internet.

Microsoft Office Programs

One of the major advantages of working with **Microsoft Office** to create web pages is that you can use (most of) the commands and techniques in the same way as you would if you were producing a non-web page.

Although not all of the features of the programs are available for creating web pages, most are, and you can use many of the multi-media techniques as well (for example you can add sound or movie clips to your page).

Be **very** careful if you decide to add sound or visuals to your page, as they are demanding on system resources, both yours and the person downloading your pages.

Remember that some people downloading your pages may not have the very latest technology and may be working with slow modems and (even) text only browsers.

Word 2000

Word

You can create a web page in various ways; each will be described in turn.

Starting A New File

When you select **File**, **New**, **More Web Templates** and then **Web Pages**, there are various buttons to help you create your web site.

This section deals initially with the **Web Page Wizard** and then with the other choices.

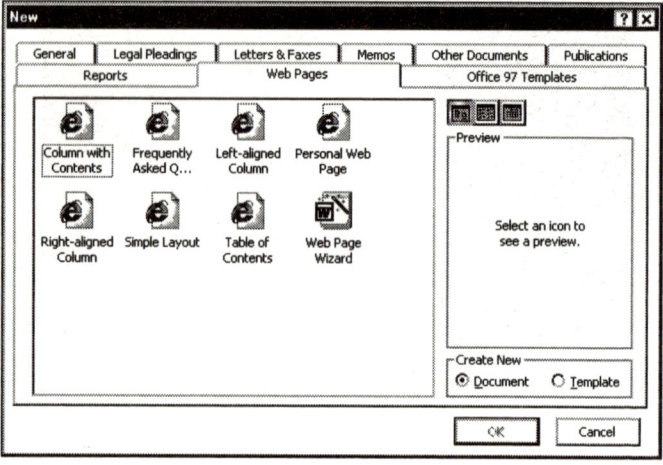

Web Page Wizard

This automates the procedure for creating a web page.

> You can use any of these techniques in your own web pages by using the pull down menus e.g. the **Format** menu and then you can apply themes to your page by selecting **Theme**.

The wizard takes you through several steps; you make choices within these and end up with a web site that contains text and pictures that you replace with your own content.

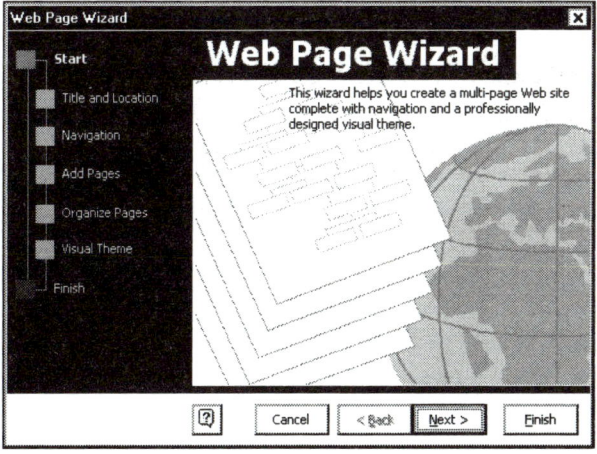

The following screen requires you to name your web and choose which folder you want to save it in.

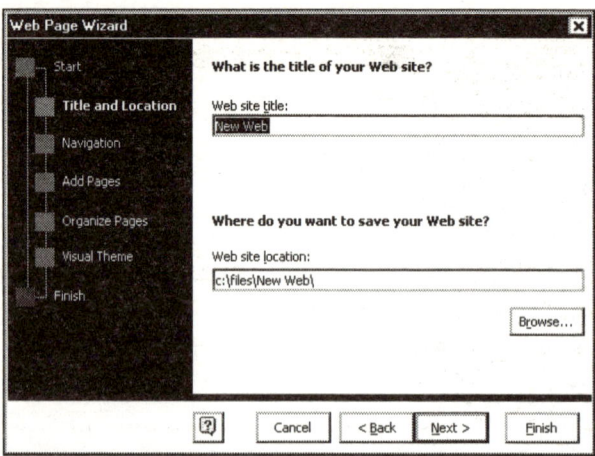

The next screen offers you the choice of creating a frame-based web or individual pages linked by navigation buttons.

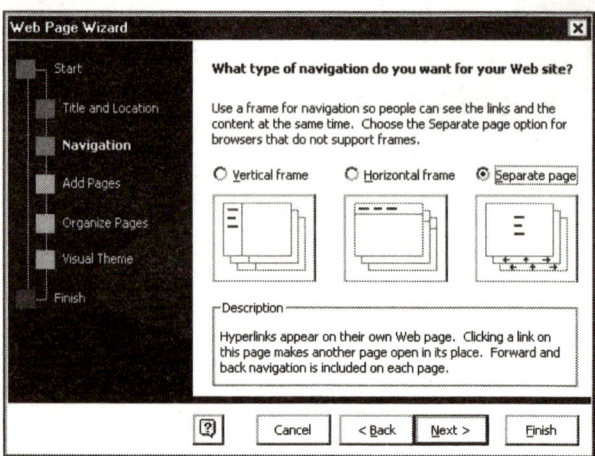

A screen enabling you to add pages to the web follows this. The wizard creates a personal site (as you can see from the first page in the list).

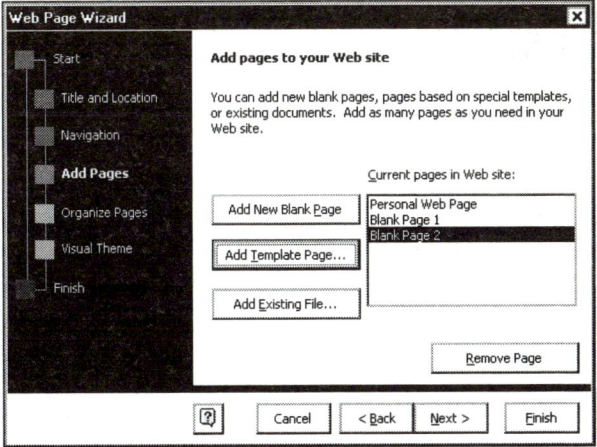

The new pages can be **Blank Pages** or **Template Pages** (using one of the **templates**; the choices are shown in the illustration on the next page).

Alternatively you can add an **Existing File**, e.g. a Word document, an existing web.

Use the **Remove** button to delete any unwanted pages

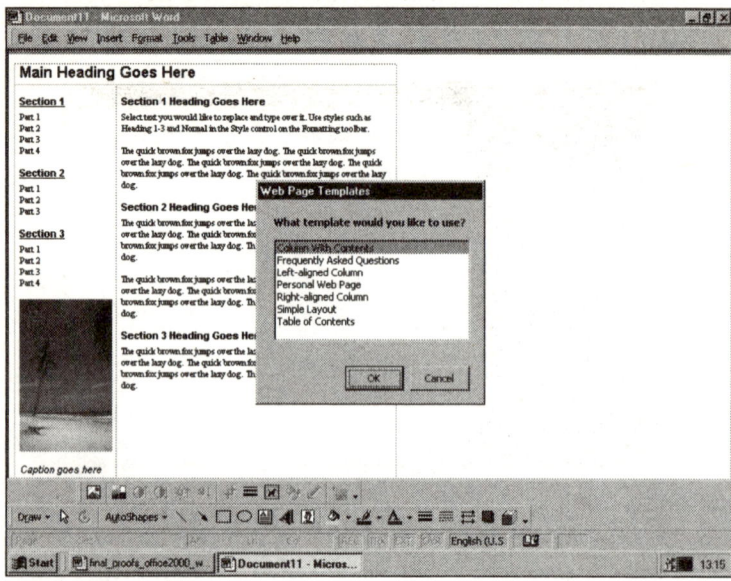

You can alter the arrangement of the pages on the next screen.

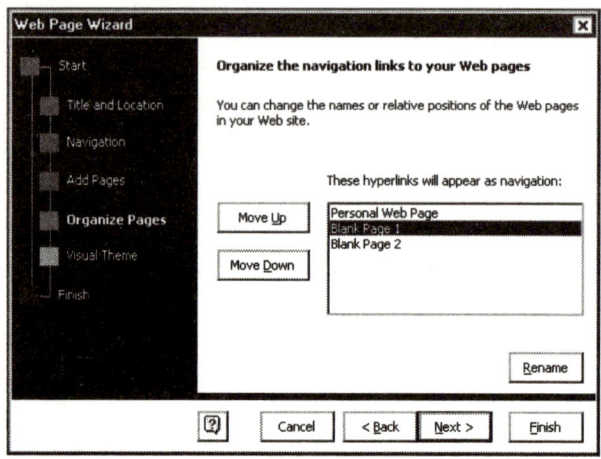

If you want to add some colour and variety to your web site, you can add a visual **theme** using the next screen in the wizard.

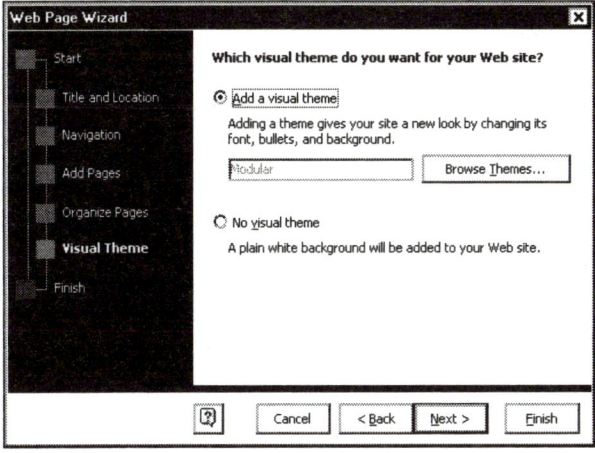

The choice of themes is shown below.

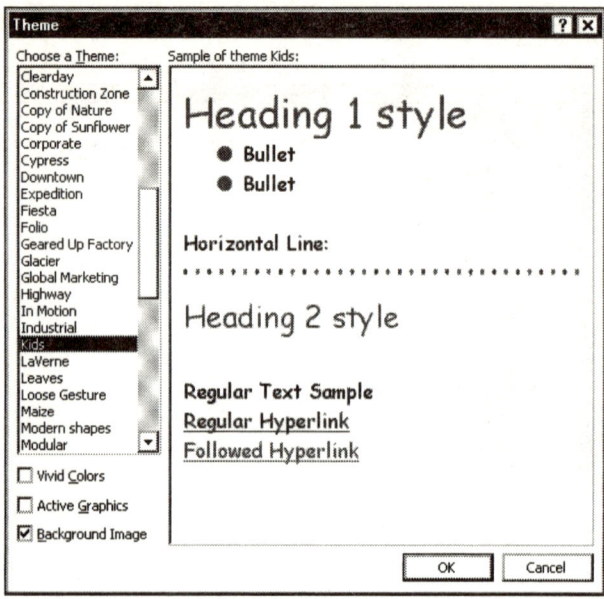

There is a final screen (which tells you that the wizard is finished) and that you have completed your web site.

You replace the text and images with those of your own and move from one page to the next by using the *underlined* hypertext links.

Here is an example of the finished result.

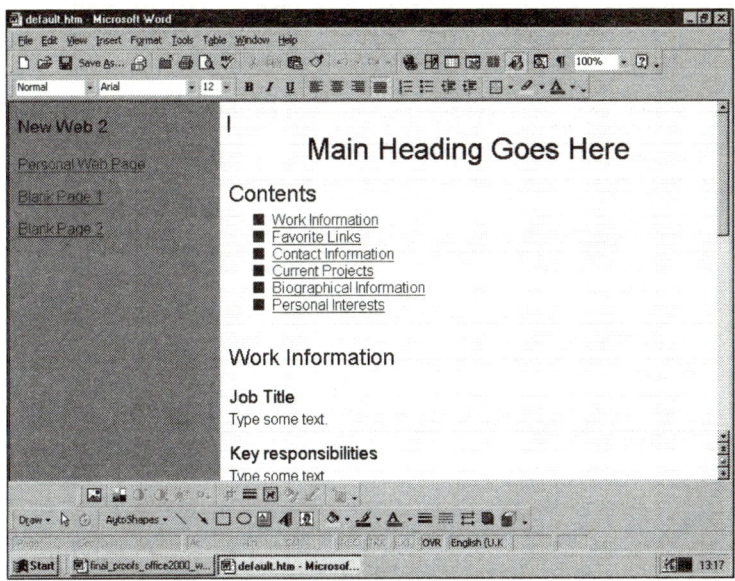

You can view the page in the browser by clicking on **Web Page Preview** (in the **File** pull-down menu).

You will be prompted to save the file before viewing it in the browser.

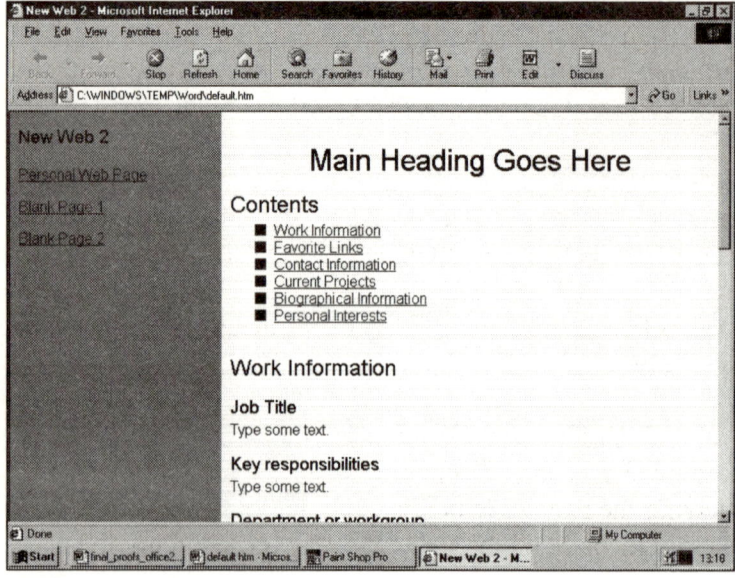

Using a browser

To see how the page will really look and how the links work, it is best to view the pages in a browser such as **Internet Explorer** (you can use this off-line without incurring any telephone or ISP costs).

This is necessary, as the page may not look precisely the same within the Office program and the browser. You should test your pages in as many browsers as possible so that you can ensure the greatest possible viewer satisfaction (nowadays this probably means **Explorer** and **Netscape**).

Another variable is the resolution you have on your display and the size of the screen, please remember that the person viewing the page may not be using 800 x 600 resolution on a 17" screen although this tends to be the standard now.

Other web page choices

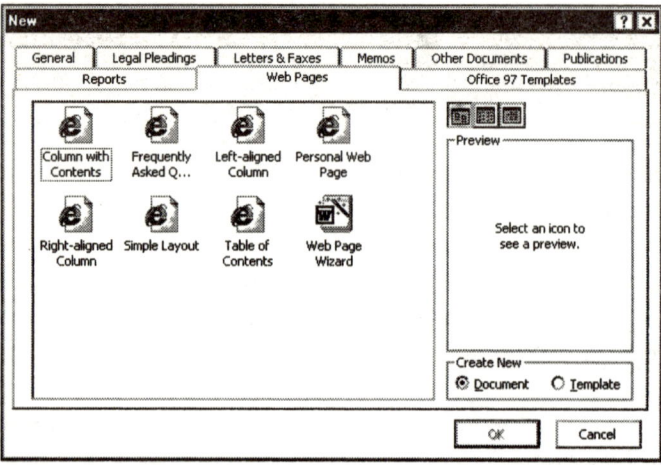

Instead of using the wizard, you can select any of the other web page layouts beginning with the very basic (**Simple Layout**), which provides text without links (you simply change the text as necessary).

Some of the more sophisticated templates contain links to different sections within that page. An example is shown below (**Frequently asked Questions**).

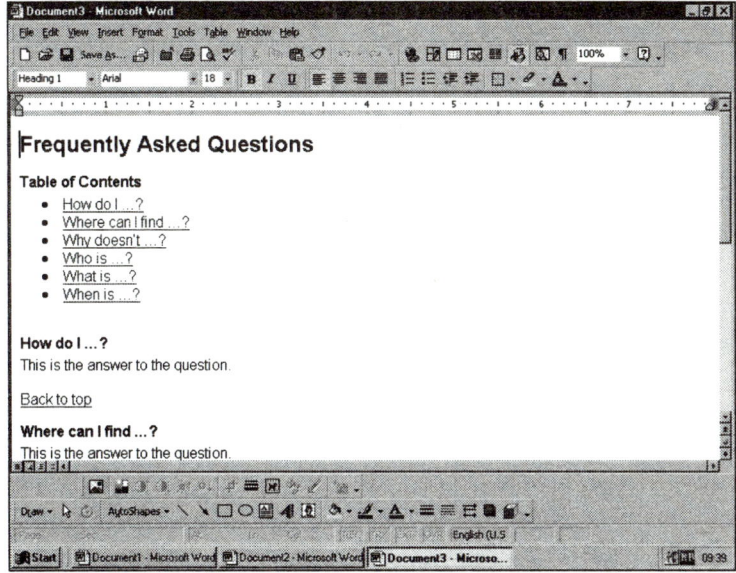

Word files

Another option is to create your page as a normal Word document and then save it as a web page (**File** menu and then **Save As Web Page**).

Some features of Word are not supported by HTML.

This is quick and easy but the results may not be as good as designing a web page properly, however you can alter them afterwards.

An example of a word document converted to HTML is shown on the next page, as you can see it is not as impressive as using one of the web templates and will require some work to turn it into an interesting web page.

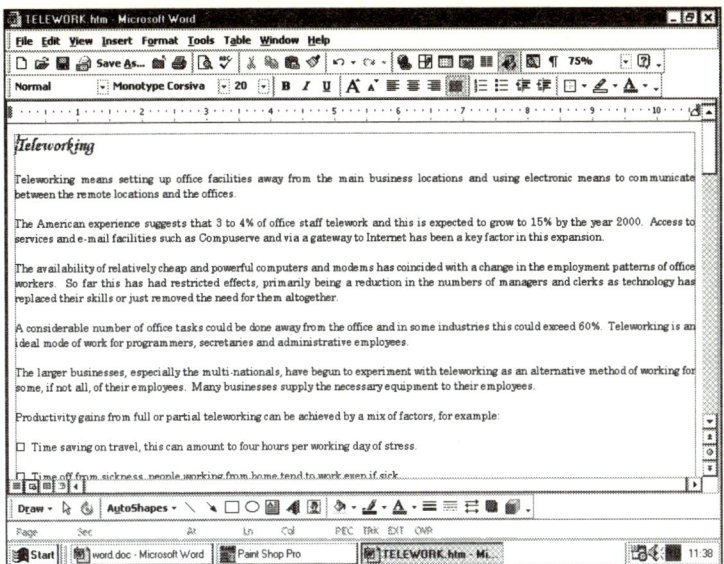

However if you want to create a different look and feel then this is a possible starting point.

Working with the source code

If you are familiar with HTML code then you can alter parts of the code, to do this pull down the **View** menu and select **HTML Source**.

The screen will display the code and you can edit this and save the results, before returning to the original screen.

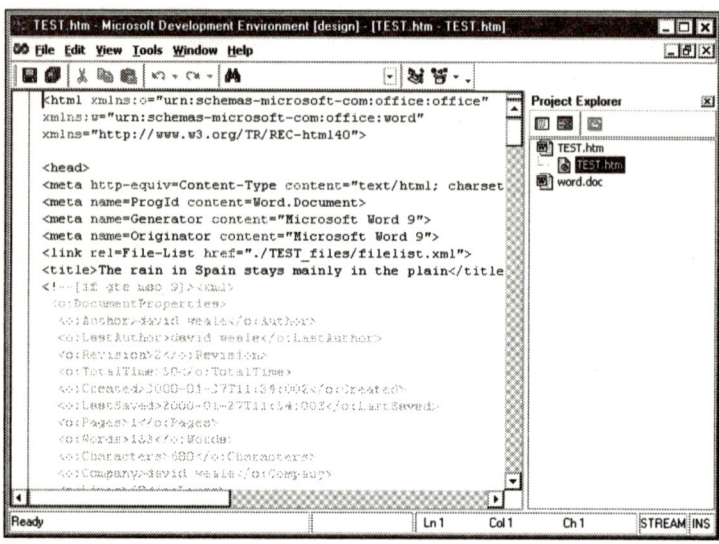

It really is worthwhile having an understanding of HTML as it allows you to alter or adjust the pages very effectively.

There is a section on HTML coding later in the book.

Working with Word

Before starting, you need to decide how you are going to create your pages.

- One way is to enter all the text and pictures and then to format them.

- Alternatively, you can format the text as you enter it; this has the advantage of enabling you to see the page as it is created.

Whichever method you choose, there are many techniques you can use to enhance your work.

Here are some of the most useful and immediate techniques for dealing with text and graphics, others are dealt with later.

Text

Fonts

You can alter the size and type of font; make it bold, italic and so on (remember that there are buttons for **bold**, *italic* and underline, etc., on the toolbar).

The alternative to using the toolbar buttons is to pull down the **Format** menu and select **Font**.

To alter any text you must first highlight it.

Text colour

You can change the text colour (after selecting the text by highlighting it) by using the **Font Color** button. If you click on the button, the text will alter to the colour shown.

If you want to alter it to another colour simply click on the arrow to the right of the button and you will see a display of the colours available.

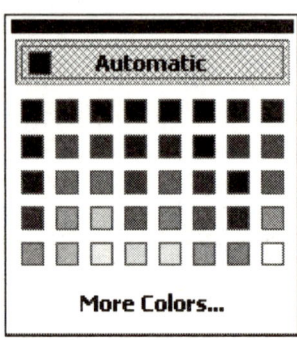

Highlighting

To the left of the **Font Color** button is the **Highlighting** button; highlight by dragging it across the text (after selecting the colour by clicking the arrow to the right of the button).

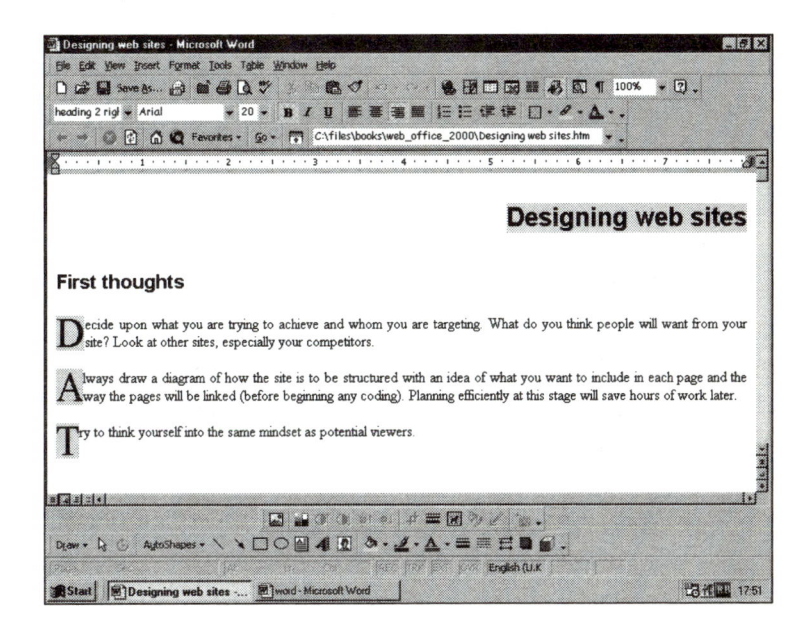

Alignment

Similarly, you can align the text using the alignment buttons on the toolbar.

Lists (bullets and numbering)

You can create numbered or bulleted lists of text. To do this you may either:

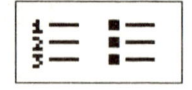

❑ Highlight the list and add bullets or numbers to it or

❑ Begin a list with a bullet or number and then add to the list by using the return key to move on to the next item in the list. If you choose this method, you need to hit the return key twice to end the creation of bullets or numbers.

If you want more variety, try pulling down the **Format** menu and selecting **Bullets and Numbering**. Note the **Picture** button (within the dialog box), you can use a variety of bullets or you can use any image as a bullet.

Background colours

Your page background can be of any colour, pull down the **Format** menu followed by **Background**.

The page will take on that colour or **Fill Effect** (containing many interesting patterns and textures, or you can import your own).

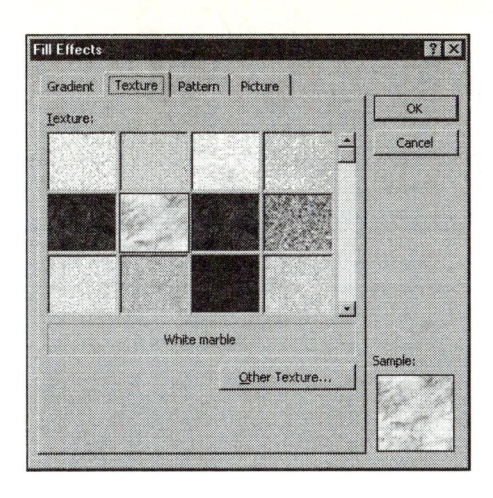

Be careful with your choice of text and background colours, it is possible to create a page that is pretty but unreadable.

A coloured background may be easier for the viewer to read.

Try for a contrast between the text and the background, dark type on a light background or vice versa may work well.

Working with graphics

Graphic images are a very important element of your pages. The advantage of the Internet over traditional information systems is that you can use any combination of graphics, text formatting, sounds, movies and colours to make your message more professional, attractive and informative.

To insert a picture, pull down the **Insert** menu and select **Picture** (either from a **File** or from **Clip Art**).

Web pages can only support a limited range of graphic file formats; the most popular are **GIF** and **JPEG**. Both have advantages and disadvantages in terms of image quality and file size (speed of download).

Once the graphic has been inserted into the page, you can modify it in various ways.

Aligning graphics

Select the image by clicking on it, then pull down the **Format** menu, and select **Picture** (or **right click** the image with the mouse and select **Format Picture**).

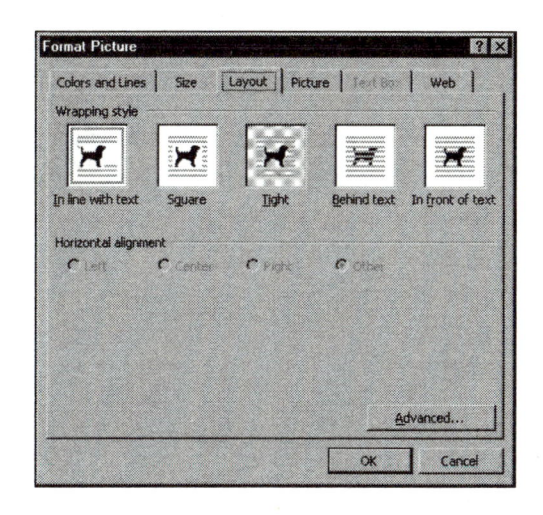

You can choose to **Wrap text** around the graphic.

With some of the wrapping styles you can also alter the distance from the graphic to the text by using the **Distance from text** measurements using the **Advanced** button (either by typing them in or by using the arrows to the right of each measurement).

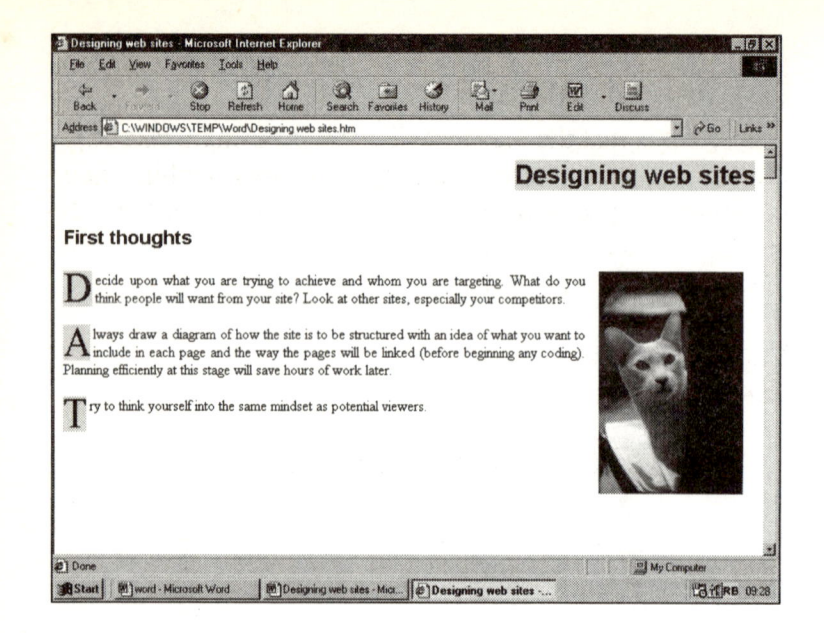

Using the Picture toolbar

It is easier, if you are working with graphics, to use the **Picture** toolbar instead of using the pull-down menus.

To display the **Picture** toolbar, pull down the **View** menu and select **Toolbars**. Click on **Picture** (so that there is a tick by it) and the toolbar will be displayed.

The toolbar contains the **Text Wrapping** button, the **Format Picture** and **Insert Picture** buttons and the **Reset** button (which resets the picture to its previous dimensions).

Text only browsers

It is possible that the viewer will either be using a text-only browser or have turned off the pictures within their browser. It is therefore sensible to enter some text that will appear in place of the picture so that the viewer has some idea of what the image showed.

You can do this by using the **Web** option within the **Format Picture** option.

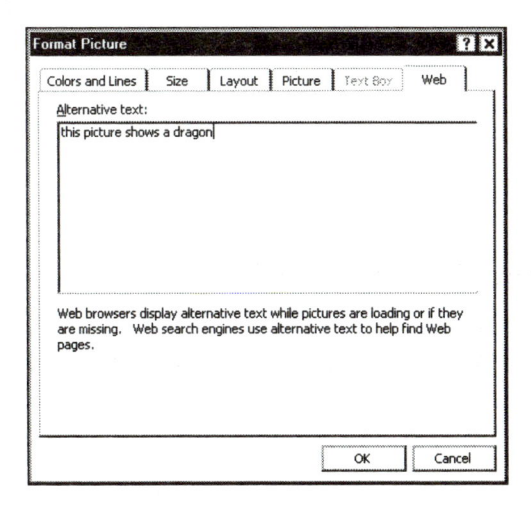

Hyperlinks

The way in which you move from page to page (or within a web page) is to use **Hypertext** links.

To create a hypertext link is simple. Type in the text you want to appear, highlight it and then click on the **Insert Hyperlink** button and enter the name of the HTML file you want the link to point at.

The dialog box is shown below.

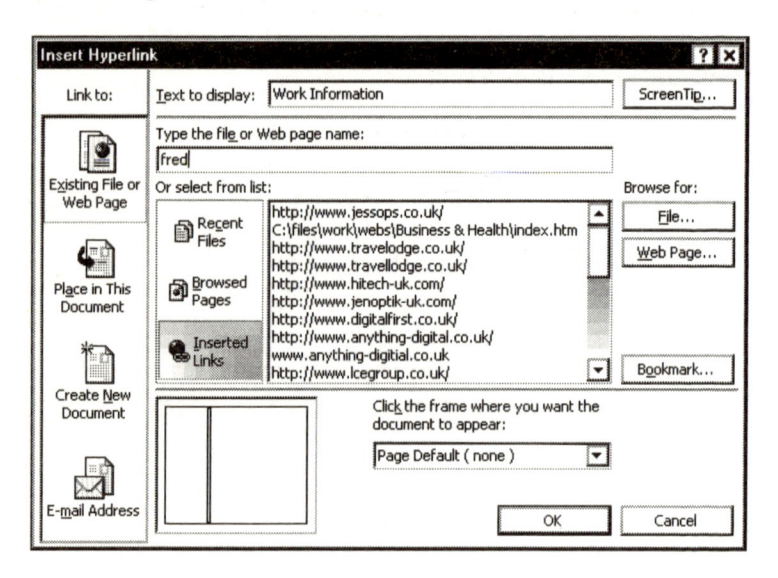

Bookmarks

If you insert bookmarks into a web page, you can use them in two different ways.

❑ Insert hypertext links within the page itself, so that the link is to another part of that page (rather than to another web page).

❑ When you create a link to another page, you can make the link jump to a section within the page.

To insert a bookmark, position the cursor at the point in the file where you want the bookmark, pull down the **Insert** menu and select **Bookmark**.

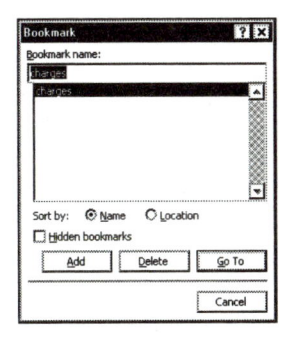

Type in the text you want to use to describe the bookmark and then click on the **Add** button.

Web Tools and Multi-media

The **Web Tools** toolbar has three multi-media features, video, sound and scrolling text.

Movie

It is possible to add video pictures to your web page although this is processor and memory intensive and may take a long time to download.

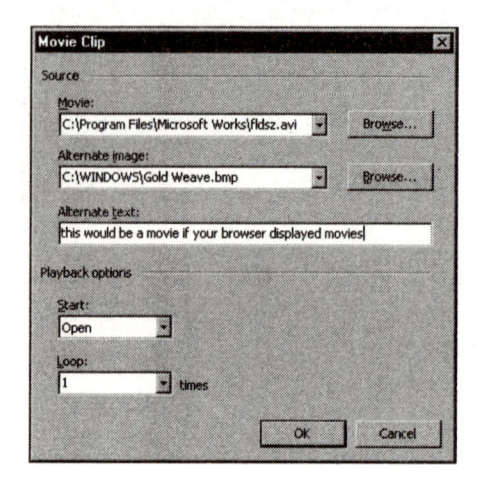

Alternative Image/Text

It is always best to add a (static) image and alternative text for those browsers that will not display movies; at least the viewer has some idea of what they are missing.

Playback options

You can begin the video when the file is loaded, when the mouse is moved over the image or both. The video can be looped any number of times.

Sound

In a similar way, you can add sound to your web pages.

This will only work where the viewer has multi-media capability. This may apply to most home users but not necessarily to business users.

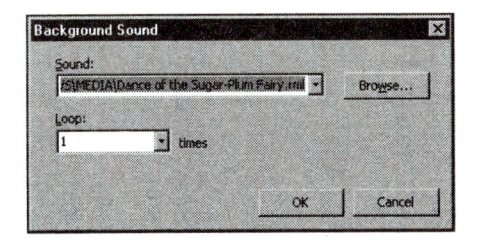

As this is a background sound, it does not show up on the page. To alter it you need to click the **Sound** button on the **Web Tools** toolbar.

Scrolling text

This is sometimes called a **Marquee**. The dialog box is simple to use.

Enter your text and the various options, a sample is shown within the dialog box.

To alter the font, click on the banner once it is in the page and you can then alter the font type and size as you wish.

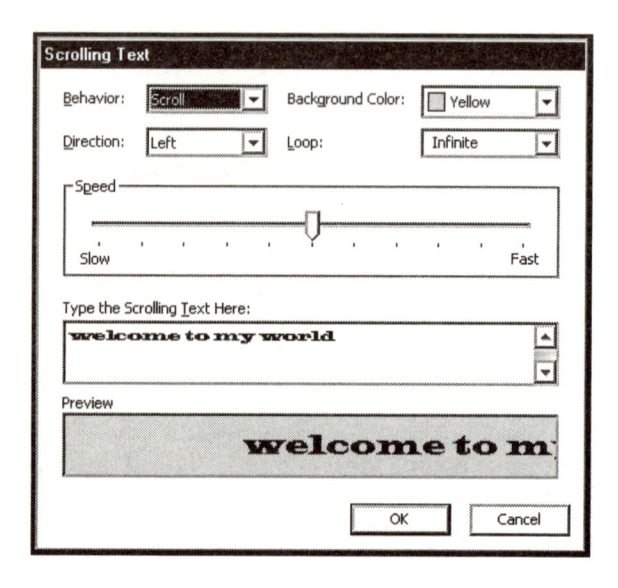

Creating Forms

Forms can be used in web pages to collect data.

If you want to design an original form, then you need to use the **Web Tools** toolbar and click the **Design Mode** button.

Form design mode

Selecting the **Design Mode** button enables you to design forms for use within your web pages.

The section on HTML looks at the various components in more detail and you can either enter the code or use the **Web Tools** toolbar (if it is available within the application) to insert the elements into your form.

The Pull-down menus

This section deals with the commands that are different from the normal **Word** menus or are especially relevant to web pages and have not been dealt with in the initial sections.

File menu

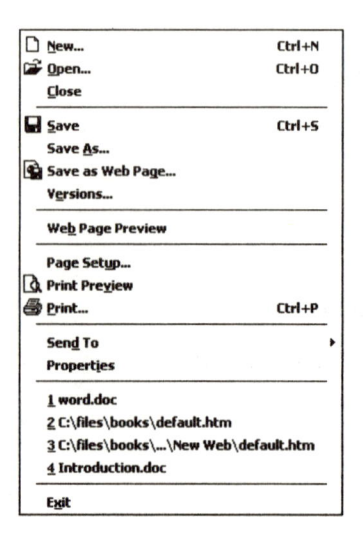

```
New...                            Ctrl+N
Open...                           Ctrl+O
Close
─────────────────────────────────────────
Save                              Ctrl+S
Save As...
Save as Web Page...
Versions...
─────────────────────────────────────────
Web Page Preview
─────────────────────────────────────────
Page Setup...
Print Preview
Print...                          Ctrl+P
─────────────────────────────────────────
Send To                                ▶
Properties
─────────────────────────────────────────
1 word.doc
2 C:\files\books\default.htm
3 C:\files\books\...\New Web\default.htm
4 Introduction.doc
─────────────────────────────────────────
Exit
```

Save as Web Page

You can save a Word document in hypertext (HTML) format.

Web Page Preview

Selecting this will automatically display the (HTML) file within your default browser, e.g. **Internet Explorer**.

Edit menu

All the commands here are standard document commands.

View menu

These are standard commands; **Web Layout** is the default for web (HTML) pages.

Insert menu

Many of these have been dealt with earlier; the others are standard Word commands.

Format menu

Drop Cap

In the **Format** menu there is **Drop Cap**, you can include these in your web pages to create interesting effects.

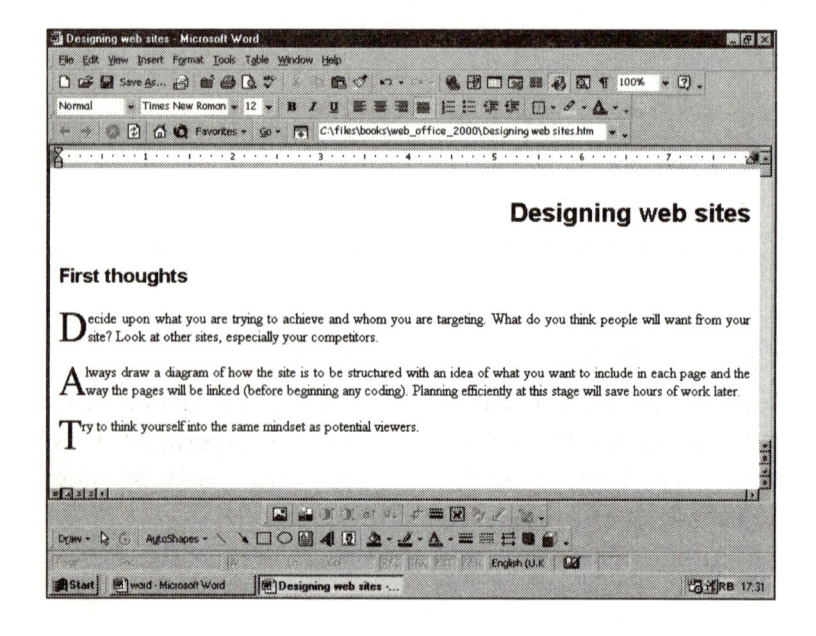

Text case

For those of us who type without always looking at the screen, there is a **Change Case** command. This is found in the **Format** menu and can save an enormous amount of time and frustration.

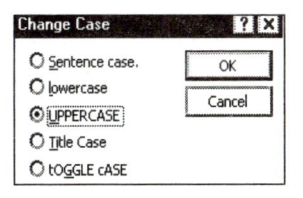

You can also use the **Shift** and **F3** buttons to similar effect.

Color and Background scheme

If you choose the **Custom** option within the dialog box, you will be able to alter the colours of the hyperlinks. This is not necessarily a good idea; your readers may become confused.

Tools menu

The **Options** command contains (within **General**) a **Web Options** button.

This enables you to make certain choices, which become the default choices. For example, you can disable features within Word that are not supported by various browsers, e.g. **Microsoft Internet Explorer** 4.0 or 5.00.

Table menu

Tables are one of the best ways of making sure text and graphics line up and look good on the page. Even if you have not used tables much before, I strongly suggest you consider using them in your web pages. For this reason I have dealt with tables in some detail.

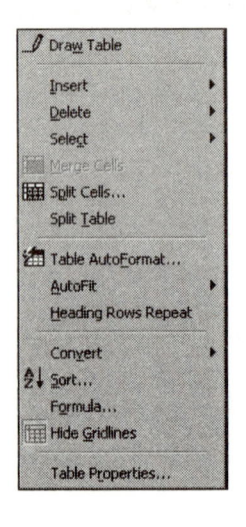

Draw Table

You can draw a table (freehand) by clicking and dragging the cursor, starting with the table and then drawing the lines for the rows and columns, the only problem is that the columns may not be symmetric.

The **Table & Borders** toolbar is displayed when you choose this option.

Here is an example I drew.

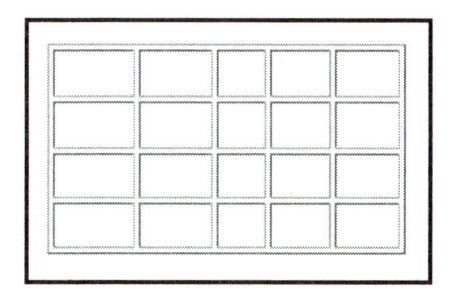

Insert

You can insert a table, a column or row or a cell (in an existing table), some of these options only display after you have created a table.

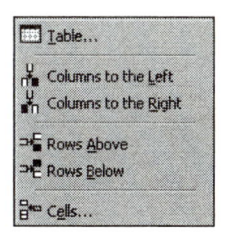

Table

This lets you specify the layout of the table (you can also click the **Insert Table** button shown opposite to select the structure by clicking and dragging over the required number of cells).

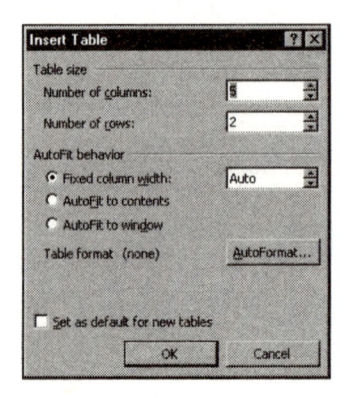

Any table you insert will appear at the current cursor position.

Here is an example of tables within tables.

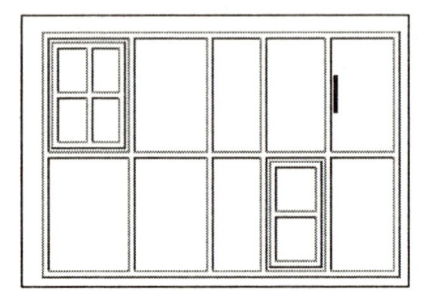

Row or Columns

You can insert rows or columns into your table at the cursor position (if you highlight several rows or columns then this number will be inserted).

Cells

This inserts additional cell(s).

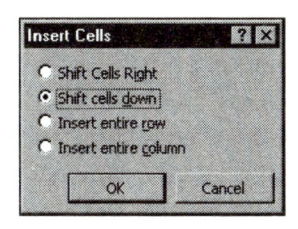

Delete Cells

This will delete the selected cells.

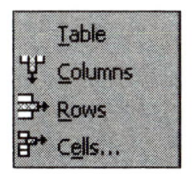

Select

You can select the whole table, a column (or columns), a row (or rows) and a cell (or cells).

Merge Cells

The selected cells will be merged into one cell.

Split Cells

This splits a cell into two.

Split Table

This splits the table at the cursor position.

Table Autoformat

You can use this to apply various formats to the table (which you can alter manually later, if you so wish).

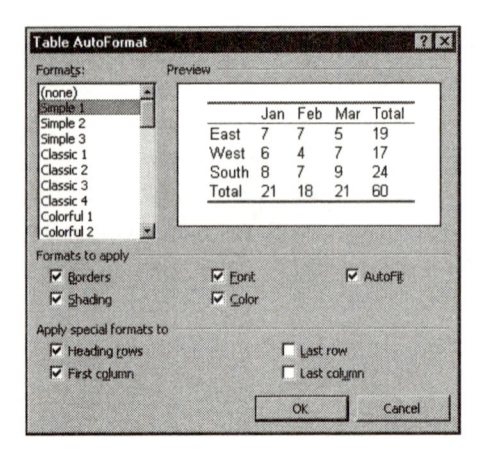

Autofit

Automatically fits the cells to the contents.

Convert

Text To Table

This converts the selected text into a table; how the text is separated into cells is defined within the dialog box.

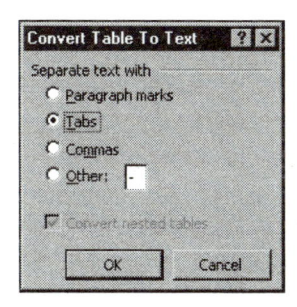

Convert Table To Text

Converts the contents of a table into text, each cell becoming a separate line.

Table Properties

You can alter various properties of the table, this is particularly useful if you want to change the alignment of the table itself, e.g. to centre the table on the page, or if you want to align the contents of cells.

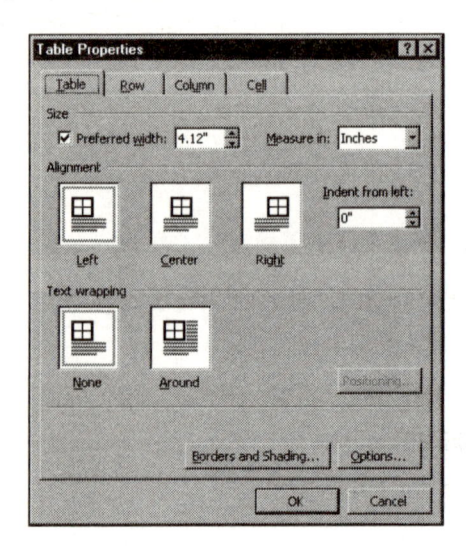

[Screenshot of Table Properties dialog box with Table, Row, Column, Cell tabs; Size section with Preferred width 4.12" and Measure in Inches; Alignment options Left, Center, Right; Indent from left 0"; Text wrapping options None, Around; Positioning, Borders and Shading, Options, OK, Cancel buttons.]

The **Size** (if defined in percentage terms) means that the table will resize to fit within the browser's window.

Note the **Options** button which enables you to alter the margins or padding within each cell.

The **Borders and Shading** button is also very useful; it is likely that you will want to use tables to lay out your pages but not to show the actual table border. To do this, choose the **None** setting within the **Borders and Shading** option.

Tables & Borders Toolbar

If you use tables often then this is a useful alternative to the pull-down menu (**View**, **Toolbars**).

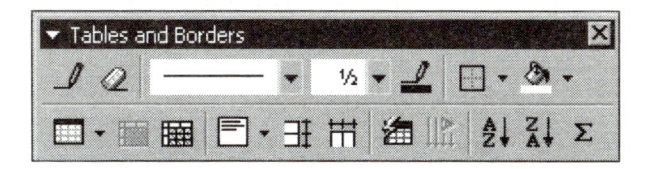

Window menu

This is the same as the standard menu.

Help menu

Similar to the normal menu.

MS Publisher

When you start the program, you are given a variety of choices from the **Microsoft Publisher Catalog**.

Wizards

Select the option **Web Sites** from the list on the left of the screen and then choose your web site layout from the choices on the right (you can scroll down to see the many different layouts).

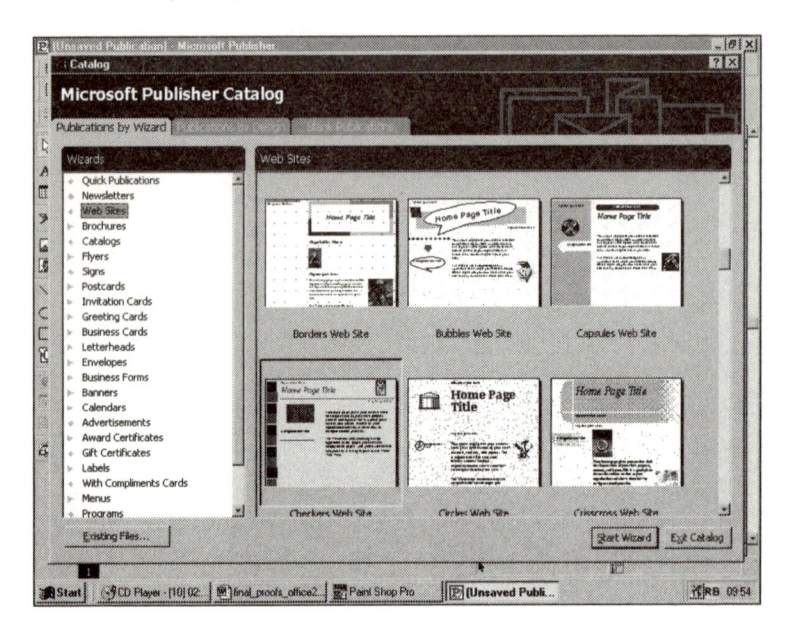

There are two options for using the **Wizard**, either of which can be chosen by selecting the **Tools** menu, clicking **Options** and then the **User Assistance** tab.

To make the choice, you may need to exit from the **Catalog**, make the changes and then pull down the **File** menu and select **New** to begin again.

The default **(Step through wizard questions)** is for you to follow a series of step-through questions, making choices at each stage.

You will end up with a completed web site into which you enter your own text and images, etc.

Alternatively
You can turn off this feature and you will then end up with a similar result but not have to make the choices.

Either way you end up with a web site which you can alter using the choices on the left of the screen.

I suggest using the step-through wizard questions until you are familiar with the program and then turn off this option.

The Step-through wizard questions

Click the **Start Wizard** button on the bottom right of the screen and the following screen will be displayed.

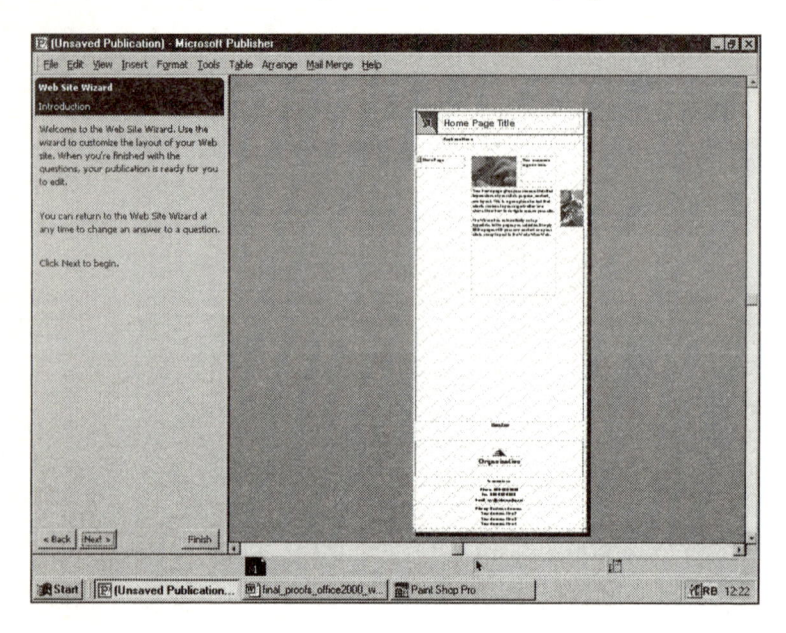

You progress through the wizard by using the **Next** and **Back** buttons on the bottom of the left-hand side of the screen.

Color Scheme

You can alter the design of your pages by selecting from the list of colour schemes.

You can select from the provided schemes or use a custom scheme that you have designed; when you choose a different scheme you will see the effect in the right of the screen.

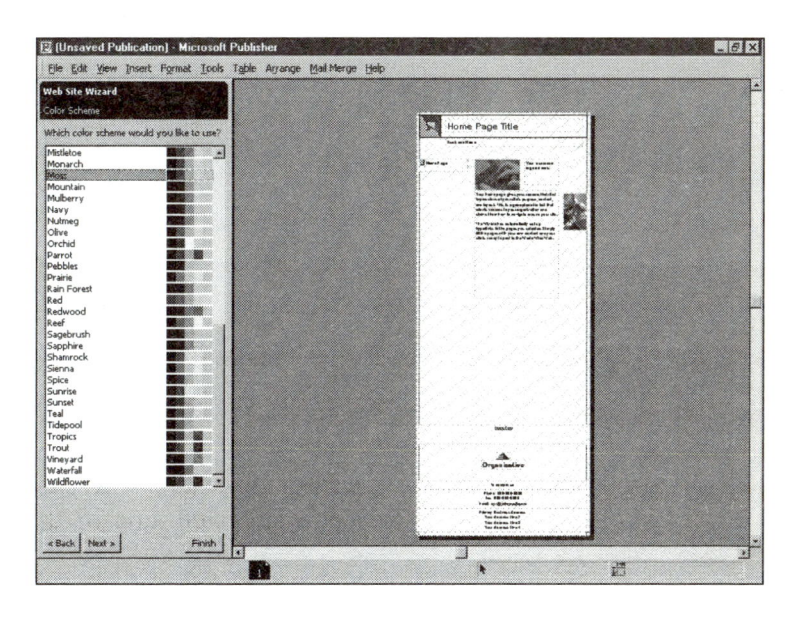

Additional Pages

On this screen you can add pages to your site from the list shown.

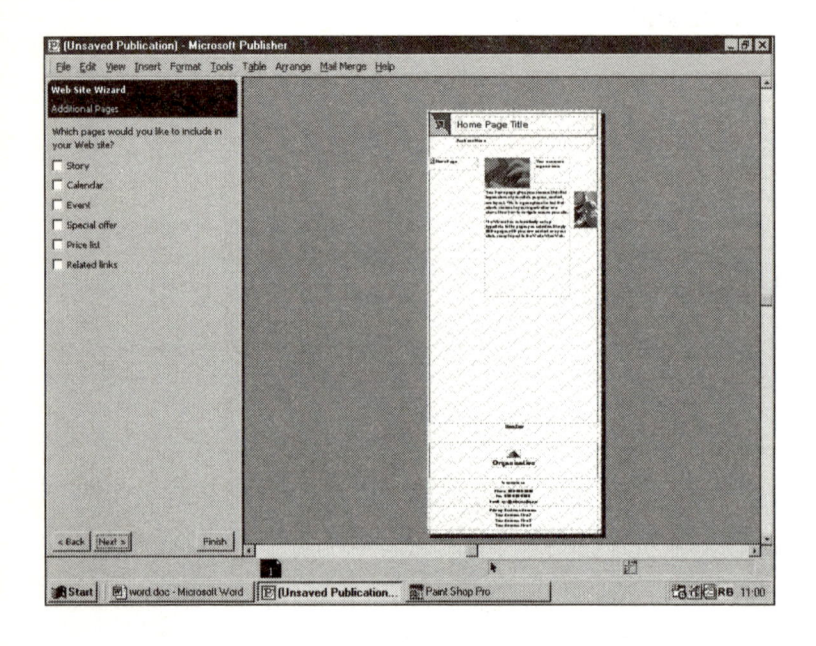

Form

Microsoft Publisher creates the forms for you (on a new page) and you can remove or alter the fields after completing the wizard.

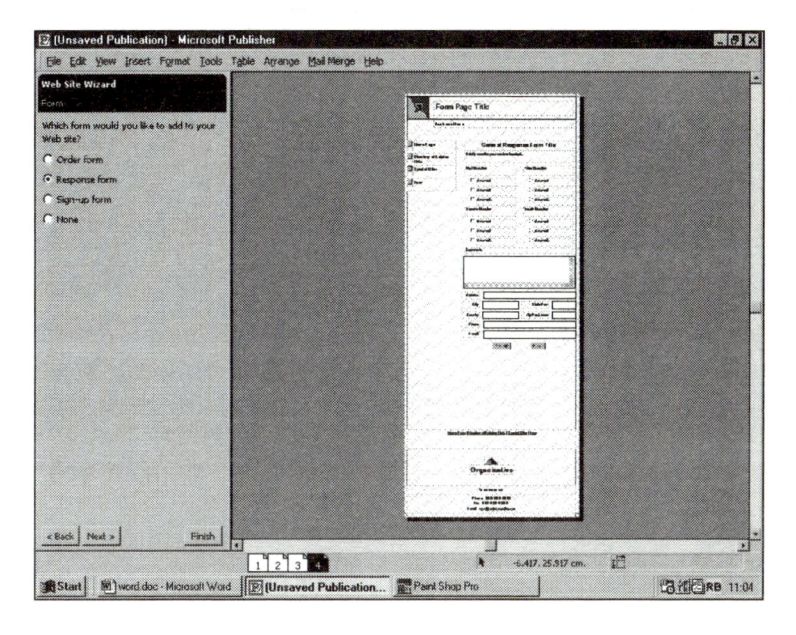

Many web sites now contain forms that can be filled in by the viewer and your ISP will return the results to you.

The HTML section of this book looks at the different types of form field you can enter.

Navigation Bar

Publisher can place a navigation bar (containing the hyperlinks to other pages) on your page.

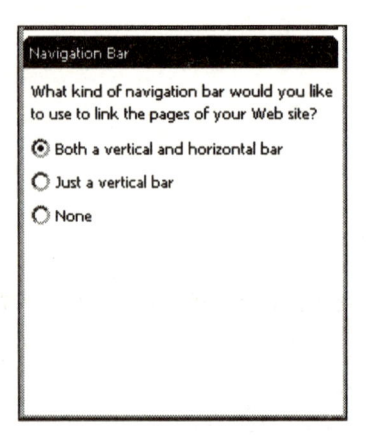

Background Sound

Publisher contains sound files; the sound will be inserted into the home page.

Background Texture

The default is to have a background texture on the pages. To remove this simply tick the **No** option.

Personal Information

You can select the type of personal information you want to include within your pages and by clicking the **Update** button, alter it.

To finish

Finally click the **Finish** button and you will be able to adjust the web site in various ways by using the **Web Site Wizard** on the left of the screen.

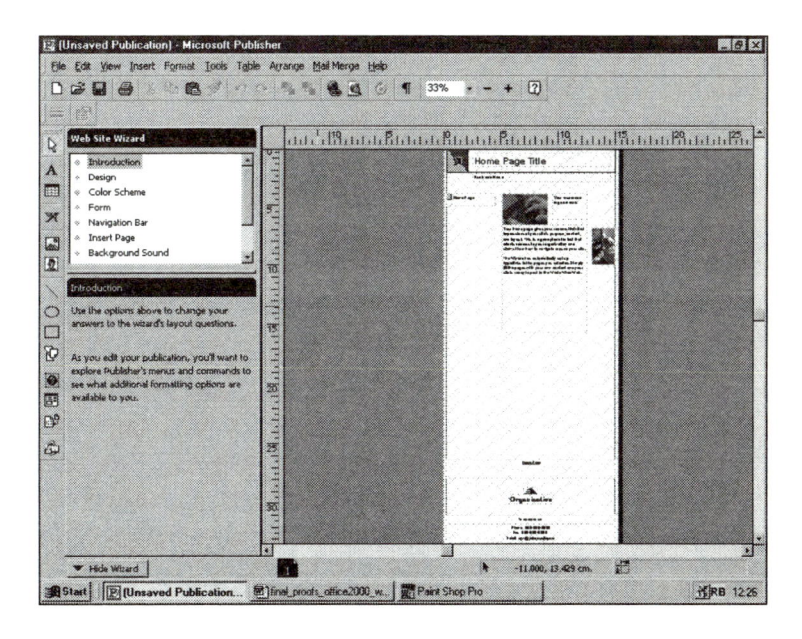

Web Site Wizard

You use the menu on the top left to make choices about the layout and contents of your web page; any choices or detail not covered previously are dealt with in the following pages.

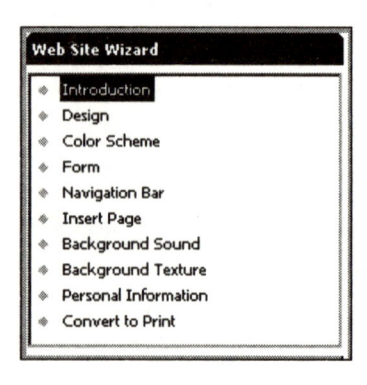

```
Web Site Wizard
  ◆ Introduction
  ◆ Design
  ◆ Color Scheme
  ◆ Form
  ◆ Navigation Bar
  ◆ Insert Page
  ◆ Background Sound
  ◆ Background Texture
  ◆ Personal Information
  ◆ Convert to Print
```

Design

You can alter the design of your pages by selecting from the list of designs.

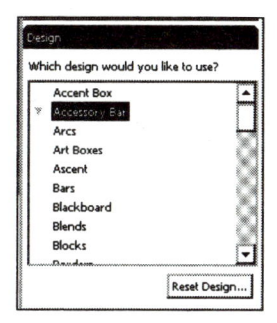

If you decide this is a mistake then you can use the **Reset Design** button, which lets you reset aspects of your choice.

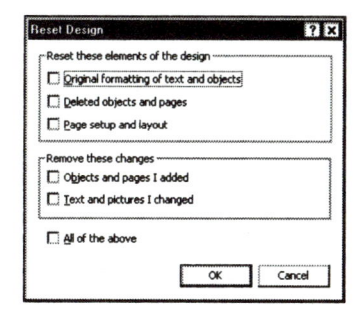

Color Scheme

You can select from the provided schemes or use a custom scheme that you have designed.

Form

You can add a form (or another form if you already have one).

Navigation Bar

Publisher can alter the navigation bar (containing the **hyperlinks** to other pages) on your pages.

Insert Page

Enables you to insert additional pages into your web. You are given choices from the pull-down list after clicking the **Insert Page** button.

The list lets you choose the contents/style of the page.

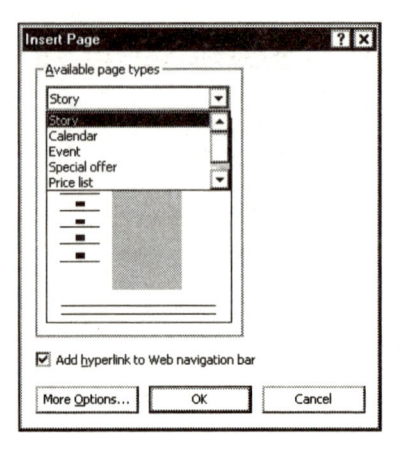

If you choose **More Options** this enables you to choose where the page is to be positioned and so on.

Background Sound

Publisher contains sound files or you can choose your own. You begin the process by clicking the **Select Sound** button.

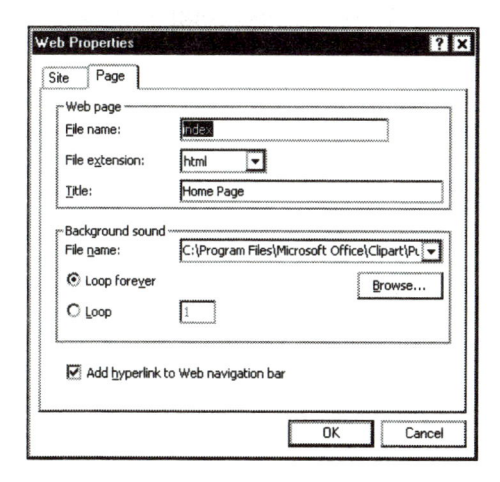

The sound will be inserted into the chosen page.

Background Texture

If you click the **Select Texture** button, you can choose a **Solid** or **Texture** background to the pages.

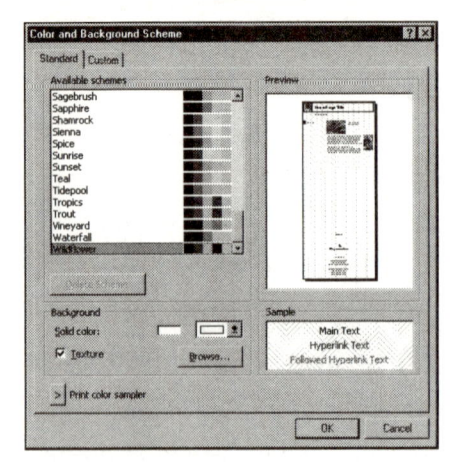

You can also customise the effects by clicking the **Custom** tab.

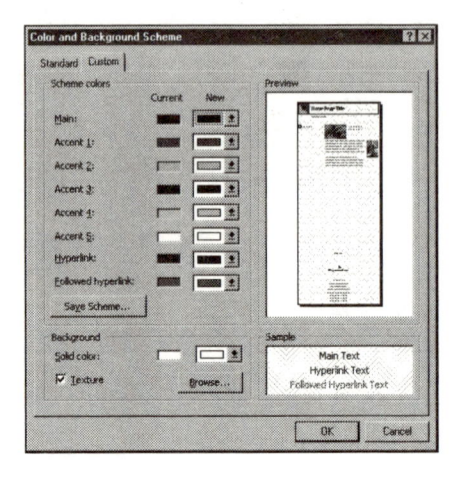

If you want a solid colour you need to deselect (remove the tick) from the **Texture** box.

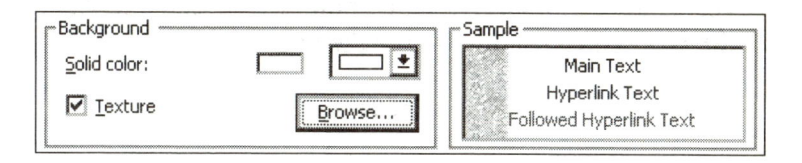

Personal Information

You can both choose the type of personal information, **Update** it and **Insert Component** (insert part or all of your personal information into a web page).

Convert to Print

You can reuse your web site as a normal publication (brochure or newsletter) if you wish.

Saving your web site

You need to save the file as a web site by pulling down the **File** menu and selecting **Save As Web Page**.

Publications by Design

While not specifically web designs, you may like to use these and then save the page as a web site, although you will need to add web features such as Navigation Bars by using the pull-down menus.

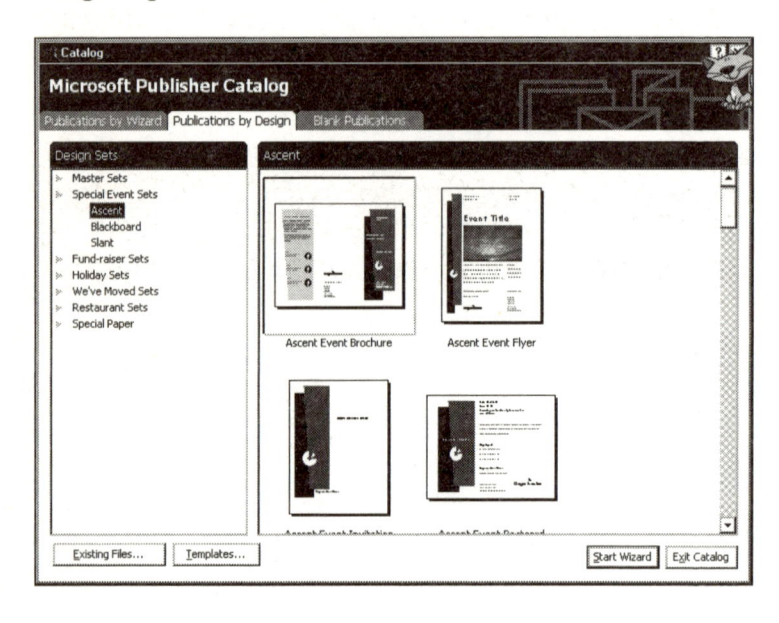

Blank Publications

Here you start with a blank page and create your web site using the various features found in the menus.

This option is in a sense the most creative and lets you fashion a unique web site (although this is not without its own dangers, especially if you do not have a good feel for or training in design).

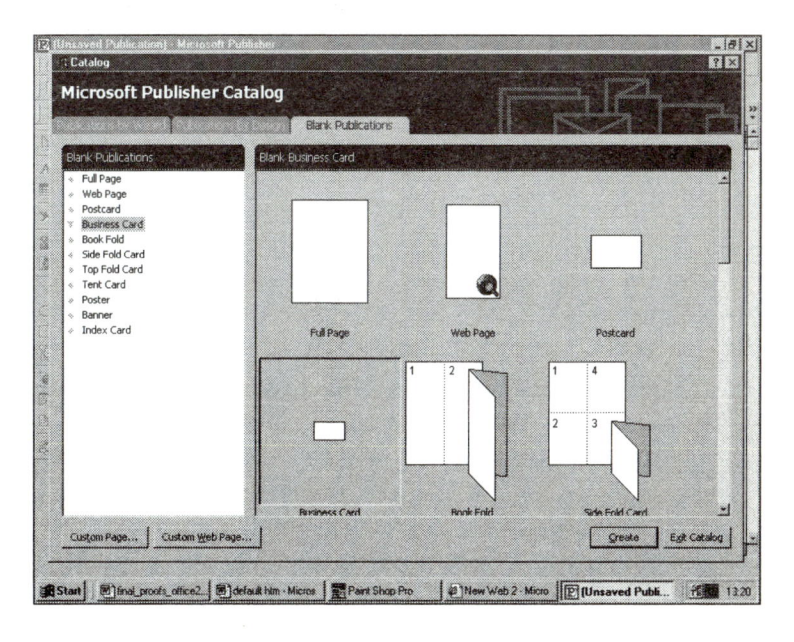

You can customise the size of the page by choosing the **Custom Web Page** option.

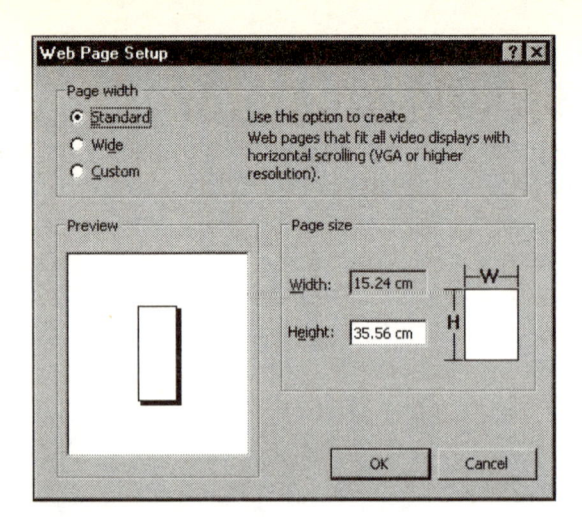

Personally I much prefer web pages not to have much need to scroll (either horizontally or vertically) and if this is also your preference then you need to adjust the default settings which give a page which extends well below the bottom of a normal screen.

Unfortunately this applies to the pages created by the wizards as well.

The pull-down menus

This section looks at the features in the pull-down menus that affect web page design.

This is not an exhaustive treatise on using MS Publisher but an overview of the web specific features.

The File menu

New...	Ctrl+N
Open...	Ctrl+O
Close	
Save	Ctrl+S
Save As...	
Save As Web Page...	
Pack and Go	▶
Web Page Preview...	Ctrl+Shift+B
Web Properties...	
Page Setup...	
Print Setup...	
Print...	Ctrl+P
Send...	

Save As Web Page

This saves your current work as a web site. Microsoft Publisher creates several files and folders during this process (rather than just a single file).

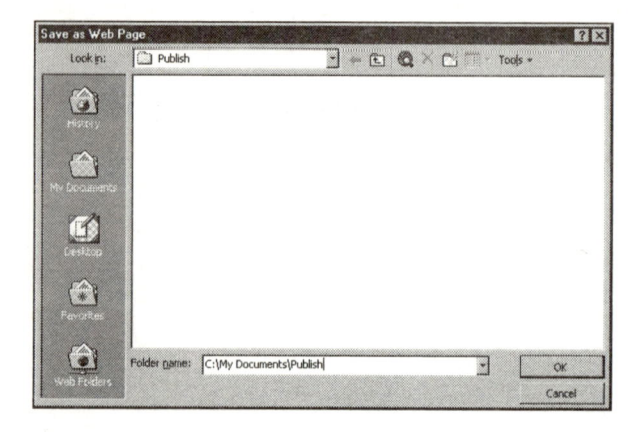

Publisher saves the web site to the folder chosen. It is important to realise that the program automatically names the pages and that if you do not select a new folder for each web site then the previous one will be overwritten.

Web Page Preview

This loads your web browser and displays your page within the browser.

You can also access this by using the toolbar button.

Web Properties

Two very useful screens, the first enables you to enter keywords and a site description, which will be incorporated into **Meta tags** (used by many search engines to index your pages) without having to do the HTML coding yourself.

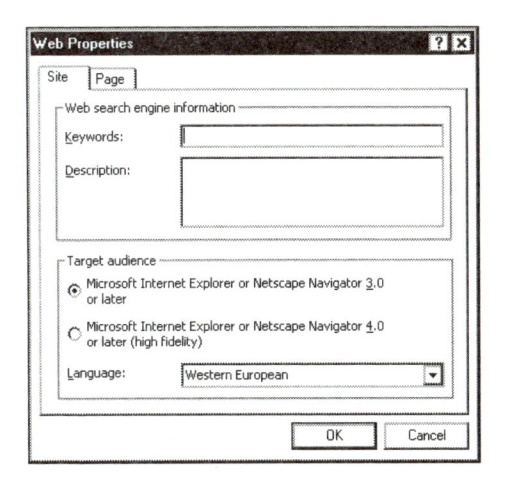

The second screen (**Page**) lets you alter the file name of the current page, etc.

Edit menu

You can edit the **Personal Information** screens from this menu.

View menu

You can display the **Web Wizard** by selecting the **Show Wizard** option. You can achieve the same by using the button on the bottom left of the screen.

Insert Menu

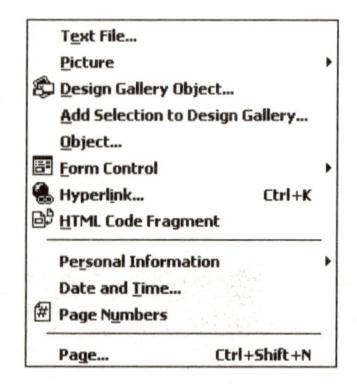

```
Text File...
Picture                              ▶
Design Gallery Object...
Add Selection to Design Gallery...
Object...
Form Control                         ▶
Hyperlink...              Ctrl+K
HTML Code Fragment

Personal Information                 ▶
Date and Time...
Page Numbers

Page...                   Ctrl+Shift+N
```

Text File

You can insert text files (you will need to create a text frame and you may need to reformat the contents) and pictures into your web pages and they will be saved in appropriate file types when you save the web pages.

Picture

You can insert pictures from various locations, if you select **New Drawing** then the **AutoShapes** toolbar is displayed.

Design Gallery Object

Microsoft Publisher contains a large variety of designs that you can insert into your web page (and alter by ungrouping and manipulating the design).

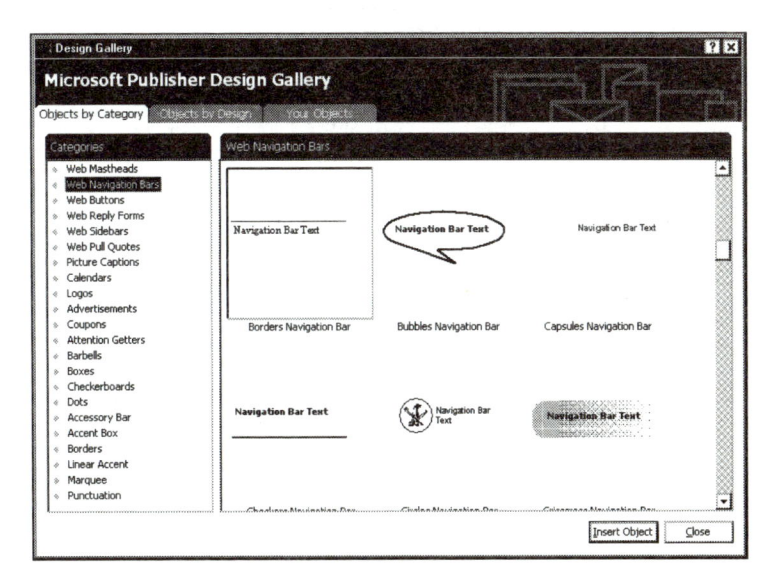

Form Control

You can create your own form design using the various boxes and buttons. The section on HTML covers the way in which form elements can be combined to create a form.

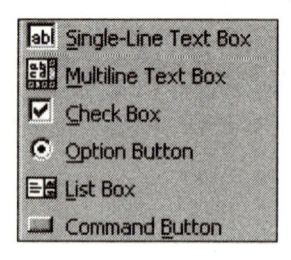

```
abl  Single-Line Text Box
     Multiline Text Box
✓    Check Box
◉    Option Button
     List Box
     Command Button
```

Hyperlinks

The essence of web pages, hyperlinks are text or graphics which lead to other pages on your site or to an external site on your Intranet or the Internet.

To add a hyperlink to another page, you need to select either an object (picture, graph, WordArt object and so on) or text.

Text/Pictures

Once you have selected the text by highlighting it or the picture by clicking it, select (**Insert Hyperlink**) or click the **Hyperlink** button and you will see the next screen.

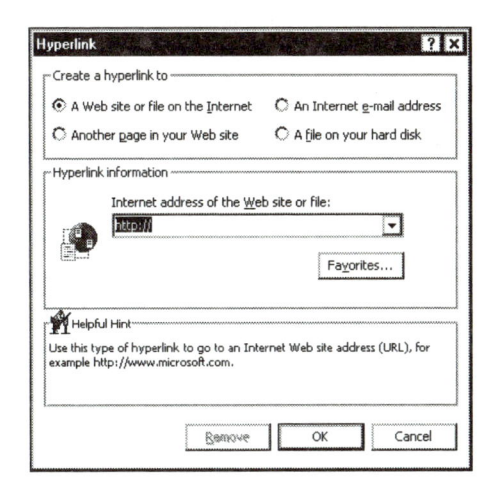

You can link to:

❑ A document already on the Internet, you need to type in the **URL** (Internet address) of the page. It is vital to enter this exactly as URL's have to precise. You may want to use the **Favourites** buttons to locate the address of a page you have looked at.

❑ Another page on your web site.

❑ An Internet e-mail address.

❑ A file on your hard disc.

Hotspots

When you use an image as a hyperlink then you can use different parts of the image as links to different web pages, i.e. you can divide the image into sections, each section linking to a different URL. These sections are called hotspots.

To create a hotspot, click on the hotspot button (**Objects** toolbar – normally on the far left of the screen).

Then simply draw a shape within the image (it has to be rectangular). The program then displays the hyperlink dialog boxes.

Try to avoid overlapping the hotspot areas.

Format menu

There are various ways of altering the look and feel of your pages. The choices vary depending upon whether you have selected text or an image.

Tools menu

You may want to use many of these tools, for example the **Design Checker** which checks your publication. The screen below shows exactly what is checked (**Options** button within the **Design Checker**).

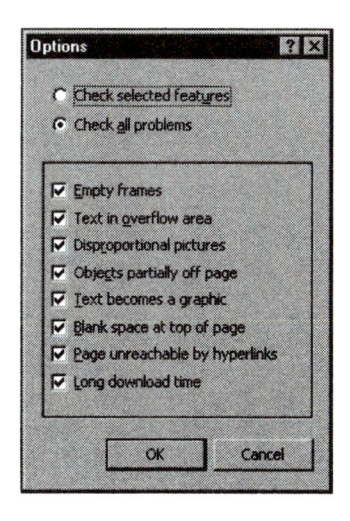

Table menu

As with the other programs, tables are a very effective and powerful layout tool.

Help menu

There is a link to the Microsoft Publisher web site, which you can use to download the latest updates.

Web Preview Troubleshooter

This contains a series of help screens, which are web specific and may assist you in problem solving and are worth a read anyway.

PowerPoint

With the growing importance and use of the Internet, the Microsoft Office programs increasingly contain web tools.

These tools enable files to be converted into a format that can be used on the Internet and company Intranets without very much work.

Using PowerPoint you can convert slide shows into web sites with a minimum of effort and time.

Saving the pages as HTML

The simplest method is to save your file as a web page. To do so pull down the **File** menu and select **Save as Web Page**.

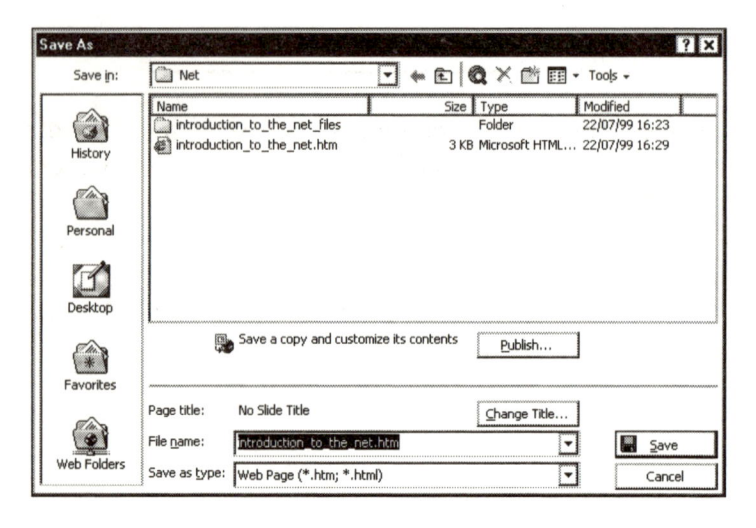

This saves the existing file as a web page (with a .HTM extension).

Alternatively, you can click the **Publish** button, which allows you to select certain options.

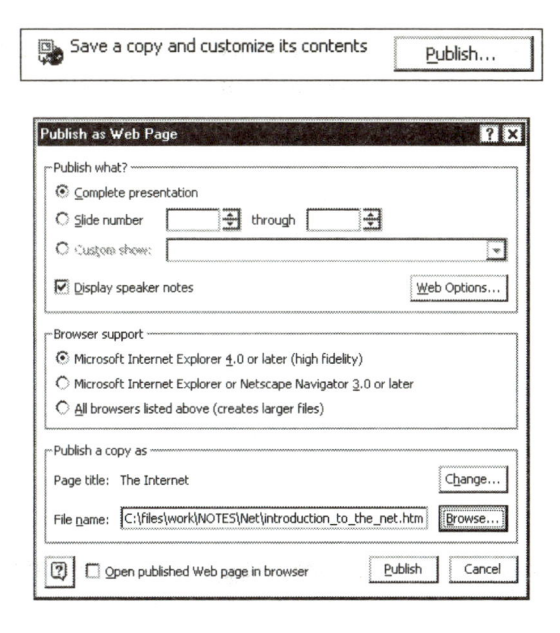

Note the option at the bottom, if you tick this then the browser will be loaded and the pages displayed without any further intervention on your part.

Once you have saved the file, you can also see how your pages will look (as web pages) by using the **File** menu and then **Web Page Preview**.

Using the browser

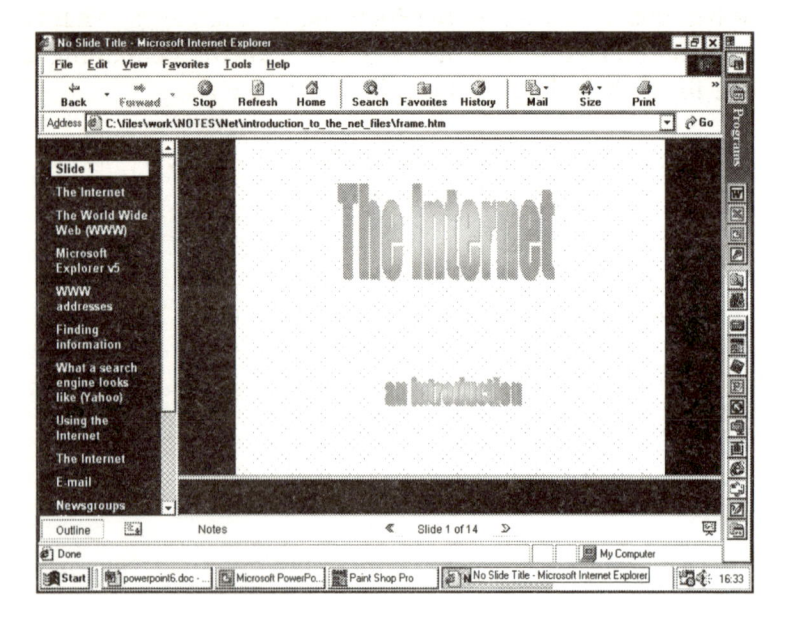

You can click the slide names (on the left of the screen) to see each individual slide (or click the arrows along the bottom of the browser screen) and you can click the word **Outline** to turn off/on the list of pages or use the button to expand/collapse the outline detail.

If the slide show has animations built into it (i.e. each line is advanced by a mouse click) then you can click the button on the bottom right of the screen which displays the slide show (rather than just the slides themselves).

Web file structure

When you save your PowerPoint file as web pages, what is actually created is a home page and a **folder** containing a file for each of the pages within the presentation.

Once you have created your web site, you can open the HTML files in PowerPoint and alter them using the normal features of the program.

Remember that if you change the HTML files, this will **not** change the original slide show, to do this you need to return to the original files, alter them and then save them again as web pages (**File** menu).

Adding links & multi-media

You can add a hyperlink to a slide. To do this, select the text or graphic for the link and click the **Hyperlink** button on the toolbar and the dialog box will be displayed.

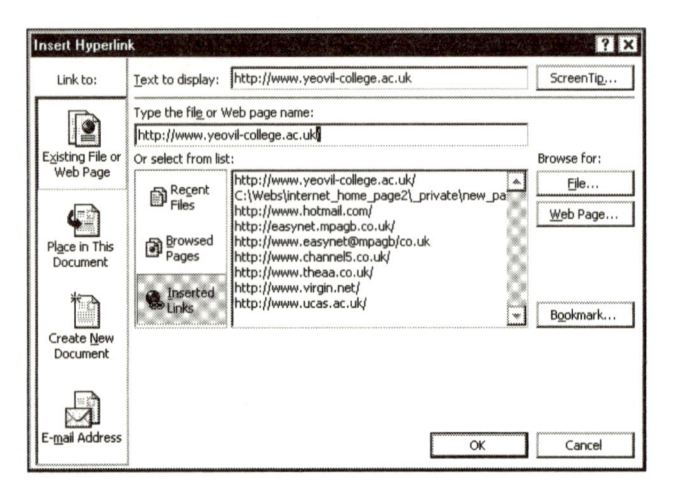

Action Buttons

You can add buttons to your slides, which are activated either by clicking the mouse on them or by moving the mouse over them.

To do so, pull down the **Slide Show** menu and select **Action Buttons**.

You choose your button from the display and then click and drag the mouse to create the button within the slide.

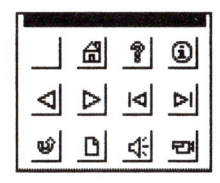

Then you enter the necessary data in the dialog box that will (automatically) appear.

You can use action buttons to jump to another slide show or web site by entering a **Hyperlink to**. This is simply the address of the slide show you want to include (either on the hard disc or on an Intranet or the Internet).

The arrow to the right of the **Hyperlink to** box will give you a choice of places you can jump to.

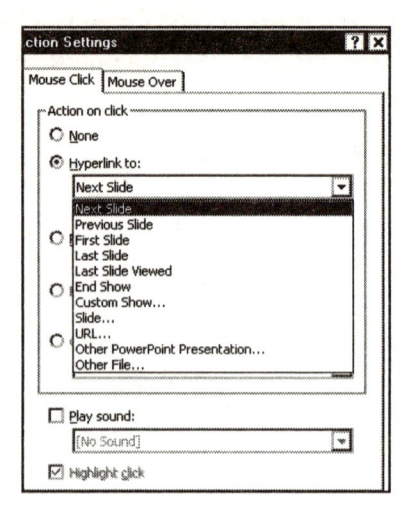

Your choice will determine the next step, for example, if you select **Other PowerPoint Presentation** then a dialog box appears enabling you to select the presentation you want to jump to.

Movies and Sounds

You can insert movie clips and sounds (**Insert** menu). There are various choices (**Gallery** refers to the **Clip Gallery**).

```
Movie from Gallery...
Movie from File...
Sound from Gallery...
Sound from File...
Play CD Audio Track...
Record Sound
```

You can add sounds in a similar way.

You will be asked whether you want the sound to play automatically or when clicked.

You can change the way in which movies and sounds are played by pulling down the **Slide Show** menu and selecting **Custom Animation**.

Other Web Applications

Microsoft Applications

Web pages and web sites can also be created using either **Access** or **Excel**. These can be integrated with existing webs or can be separate sites.

As these are a rather specialised aspect of web site creation (being based around spreadsheets and databases) they are not covered in this book.

However a brief outline of what can be achieved with them is included and anyone familiar with web design and with the use of either program will be able to learn to develop sites or pages relatively easily.

Excel

You can publish your workbooks as web pages and these can be interactive (where the viewer can make changes to the data) or not.

If you want to make them interactive then the user can enter, format and analyse the data, carry out calculations on the data and sort/filter but not change the data.

For example, if you want your user to work out interest payments, you can create a calculator for the page or you can make the pivot tables interactive so the user can rearrange the data.

Access

You can create web pages that can be used to add, edit, view, or manipulate data in a Microsoft Access database. These can be interactive or static.

Combinations

You can combine the use of the various Microsoft programs to create web pages.

For example **Access** could be used to get names, ages and salaries from a database. This data could then be analysed using **Excel** and you can add formulas that calculate the average or totals and you could then create a chart.

The result could be saved onto a web page, which could be interactive if you wanted.

You could then use **Microsoft FrontPage 2000** to add graphics and other interesting features to the pages.

Publishing your Web

You can upload your web to your ISP (internet service provider, e.g. Freeserve) either using a **FTP** (file transfer protocol) program such as **WS_FTP95LE** (which can be downloaded from the Internet) or by using the Microsoft **Web Publishing Wizard**.

> The wizard is in the **Accessories**, **Internet Tools** folder; click the **Start** button to begin.

This automates the process of uploading (sending) your pages to your internet provider. However you will need details of the address to upload to from your ISP.

HTML Tutorial

Introduction to HTML

This is an introduction to **HTML** coding, so that you can alter the code generated by the application programs such as **Word** or you can create your own web pages from scratch (which is the best way of learning about web design).

Once you have learnt HTML you will have a much better understanding of the scope and purpose of the various editors and applications you use.

In reality you will probably use an editor or application to create your pages but will be able to make fundamental changes by inserting or altering the HTML code generated by the editor or application.

Fundamentals of HTML files

All HTML files follow a fixed structure.

```
<html>
<head>
<title>an example of the use of html</title>
</head>
<body>
the contents of your page
</body>
</html>
```

The structure is created by the use of **tags**, each tag begins a different section and there is a further tag (with a / symbol) to end that part of the structure.

The main tags

\<html\>\</html\>	The file begins and ends with this tag, which defines it as an HTML file.
\<head\>\</head\>	These tags contain the title and other information.
\<title\>\</title\>	The (descriptive) title of your page is contained between these tags. Your choice of title is important, as it is shown in the title bar on browsers and can appear in search engine results.
\<body\>\</body\>	In this section, you enter the code to create your page contents.

A simple example

An example of the *body text* is shown below, which is followed by an explanation of the code.

You need to add the rest of the structure, e.g. the head section and the html tags at beginning and end as described in the illustration on the previous page.

```
<body>
<h1> david's first page</h1>
this makes use of <b>bold text</b>
<i>italic text</i>
<tt>typewriter style text</tt>
</body>
```

The tags can be capitalised or not as you prefer.

Basic tags

\<h1\>
This is a first level heading, there are six heading levels (**H1** to **H6**), **H1** being the largest.

Two examples are shown below.

\<h1\> \</h1\>	1st level heading - large, bold (with automatic line breaks and spaces)
\<h5\> \</h5\>	5th level heading - small (line breaks, etc., as above)

\<b\>\</b\>
Any text within these tags will be in bold.

\<i\>\</i\>
Text between these tags will be in italic.

\<tt\> \</tt\>
Use these if you want typewriter style text.

\<strong\>\</strong\>
Strong text (very similar to heading level 4) except that there is no line break as there is with headings.

You can combine tags, e.g. combine *italic* and **bold**.

Creating a file from scratch

1. Load Windows **Notepad** and type in the basic structure for your file.

2. Save the file as an **html** file in whatever folder you wish (add an **htm** extension to the file, i.e. **myfirstfile.htm**). It is best to make sure that the **Filetype** box shows **All Files**.

3. Close **Notepad** and load **Internet Explorer**.

4. Open the file you have just created (using the **Browse** button to locate the file).

5. Pull down the **View** menu and select **Source**; this will re-open **Notepad** with the tags shown.

6. Enter the code you want in the **body** section of the file.

7. **Save** the file and close **Notepad**.

8. Click on the **Refresh** button in **Internet Explorer** and you will see the results of your work.

9. Repeat steps **5** to **9** as necessary.

An alternative to step 4 is to drag the file from its folder into the browser or double-click it (in **Windows Explorer**).

Practice

Create a new file and enter the example described previously (**a simple example**) remembering to add the rest of the html structure.

Then view it in the browser. Call this file **ex1.htm**.

Exercise one

Create a new file using **Notepad**.

Type in the **basic structure** (html, head tags, etc.) and then add a suitable title and the following body text.

Call the file **webone.htm**

```
<body>
<h1>this is a level 1 heading</h1>
<h2>this is a level 2 heading</h2>
<h3>this is a level 3 heading</h3>
<h4>this is a level 4 heading</h4>
<h5>this is a level 5 heading</h5>
<h6>this is a level 6 heading</h6>
</body>
```

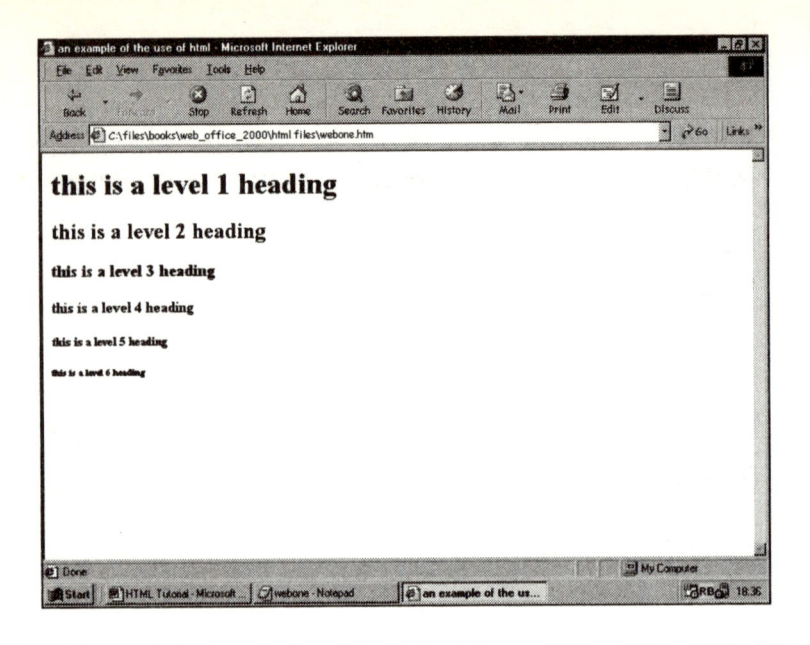

```
<html><head>
<title> an example of the use of html </title></head>
<body>
<h1>this is a level 1 heading</h1>
<h2>this is a level 2 heading</h2>
<h3>this is a level 3 heading</h3>
<h4>this is a level 4 heading</h4>
<h5>this is a level 5 heading</h5>
<h6>this is a level 6 heading</h6>
</body>
</html>
```

Formatting tags

We have already looked at some of the formatting tags (**bold**, *italic* and so on). Here are more (**n** is a number).

<u></u>
Underlining.

<pre></pre>
Pre-formatted text, any text within these tags will be laid out exactly as it appears within the tags. So, if you use tabs then these will be retained.

** **
Centres the text within the tags, note the spelling.

<font size=n></font>
The choice is from 1 (smallest) to 7 (largest). This is a relative size and will depend upon the screen resolution or the browser settings.

<basefont size=n>
This sets the default font size (from 1 to 7). The default, unless you alter it, is 3. The **<font size>** setting overwrites this.

<font color="nnnnnn"></font>
You can alter the colour of words or single characters, by entering the hexadecimal code for the colour you want.
<font color="98c2f4"> this is a kind of bluish colour.

There are sites on the Internet that display colour charts with the hex codes, which you save or print out.

<font face="name"></font>

To alter the typeface of the text, insert a font name into the tag, e.g. **<font face="arial">**

Example

This example demonstrates the order in which you need to turn on/off font settings (last font tag entered is turned off first).

Create a file called **ex2.htm** using the coding shown below and view it in the browser.

```
<html>
<head><title>nested tags</title></head>
<body>
<font size=6> <font face=arial> <font color=e2380>
the font will be size 6, in arial font and coloured red
</font>
closing the last font (color) means the text reverts back to the default colour
</font>
closing off the next font (face) means the text reverts back to the default font
</font>
closing the last font (size) means the font reverts back to the default font size
</body>
</html>
```

> the font will be size 6, in arial font and coloured red
> **closing the last font (color) means the text reverts back to the default colour** closing off the next font (face) means the text reverts back to the default font <small>closing the last font (size) means the font reverts back to the default font size</small>

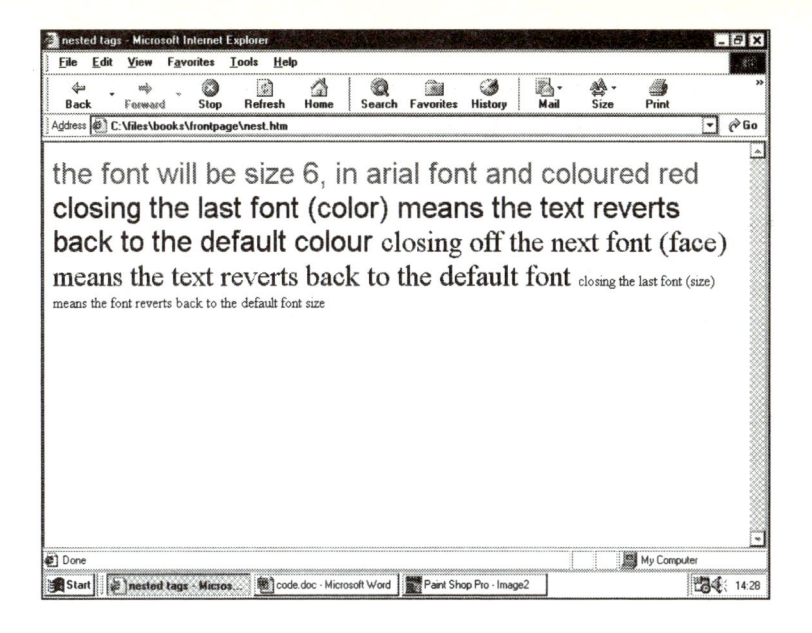

Exercise two

Create a new file called **webtwo.htm** with the following body text and formatting (after creating the basic structure of the file).

I suggest you include the tag <p> to create a new paragraph between each section. This is a stand-alone tag, which can exist without the need to turn it off.

```html
<html>
<head>
<title>exercise two</title>
</head>
<body>
<basefont size=5>this sets the default font size (1 to 7), the default is 3
<p>
<u>this underlines text</u>
<p>
<pre>
                preformatted text, any text within these tags will
                be laid out exactly as it appears, so you can use
                the tab key if you wish
</pre>
<p>
<font size=1>the smallest font, this command overwrites the basefont command until you close it</font>
<p>
<font size=7>the largest font size</font>
<p>
<font color=98c2f4>a blue color</font>
<p>
<font face=arial>this changes the font to arial</font>
</body>
</html>
```

This should look similar to the screen below.

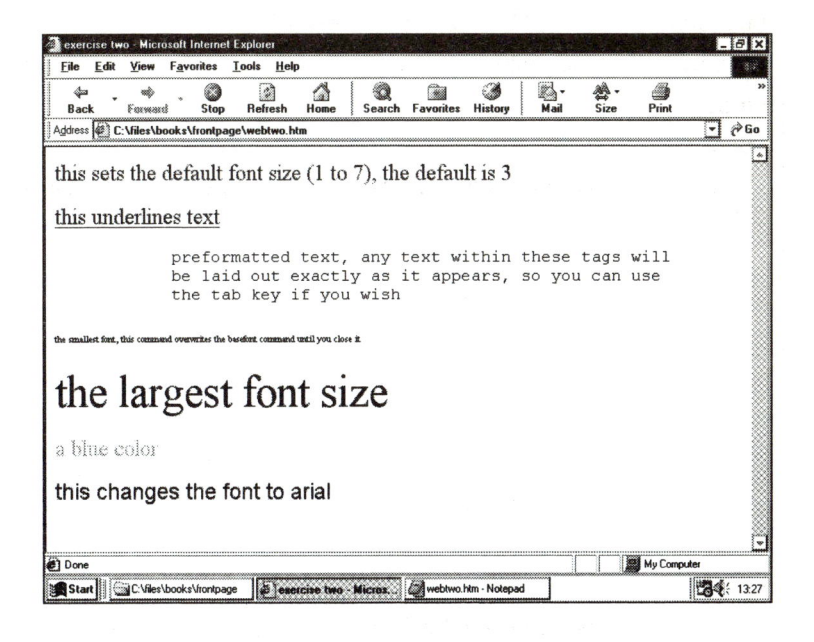

this sets the default font size (1 to 7), the default is 3

this underlines text

```
preformatted text, any text within these tags will
be laid out exactly as it appears, so you can use
the tab key if you wish
```

the smallest font, this command overwrites the basefont command until you close it

the largest font size

a blue color

this changes the font to arial

Ways of creating space(s)

The following tags allow you to create space.

<p></p>
The closing tag is not usually necessary. This tag creates a paragraph break with a space *before* the new paragraph. There is no point in adding more than one of these, as they cannot be nested.

**
**
This begins a new line with *no* line space, you can use multiple tags to add blank lines. There is no closing tag.

<hr>
Creates a horizontal line across the page.

<hr size=n><hr width=n> or <hr width=%>
Defines the size and width of the horizontal line in pixels or as a % of the page.

<hr noshade>
Produces a solid line.

<p align=center> </p>	<h3 align=left> </h3>	<hr align=right> </hr>

These commands align paragraphs **<p align= >**, or headings **<h1 align= >**, or horizontal rules (lines) **<hr align= >** and so on.

Exercise three

Open your original file (**webone.htm**) and add the following code (shown in bold) to experiment with space and the use of horizontal lines to divide the page.

Save the file as **webthree.htm** and open it in the browser.

Notice the different effects of using <p> and

```
<body>
<h1>this is a level 1 heading</h1>
<p>
<h2 align=right>this is a level 2 heading</h2>
<h3>this is a level 3 heading</h3>
<hr noshade size=50 width=50%>
<h4>this is a level 4 heading</h4><br>
<hr size=20 width=100%>
<h5>this is a level 5 heading</h5>
<br>
<h6>this is a level 6 heading</h6>
</body>
```

this is a level 1 heading

this is a level 2 heading

this is a level 3 heading

this is a level 4 heading

this is a level 5 heading

this is a level 6 heading

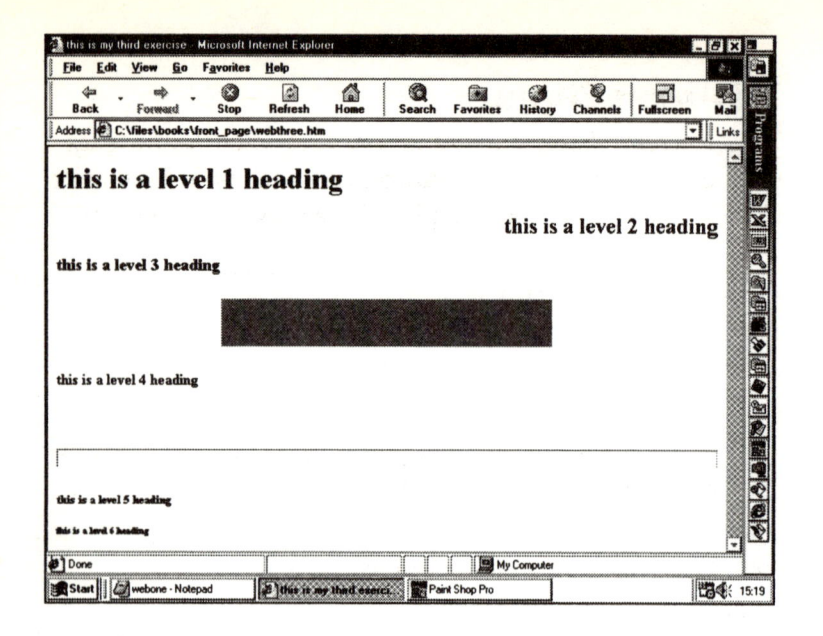

Exercise four

This exercise begins to build up your own home page. Create a new file, called **mypage.htm** and enter the details shown below. Enter paragraph or break tags as necessary.

---

title

my first home page

body

Change the font, the colour (e2380 is the hex code for red), centre this heading and make it heading level 2

Your name's home page

Heading level 4, in red and centred

created on date

revert to normal (default) text font and colour

Put in a solid horizontal line, size 10 pixels and 30% width of the page

heading level 4, colour red

address

revert to normal (default) text font and colour

type in your address using <br> to put each part of the address on a new line, there should be a new line for each part of the address

heading level 4, colour red

occupation

revert to normal (default) text and colour

type in your job title

Your page may look similar to this although please experiment.

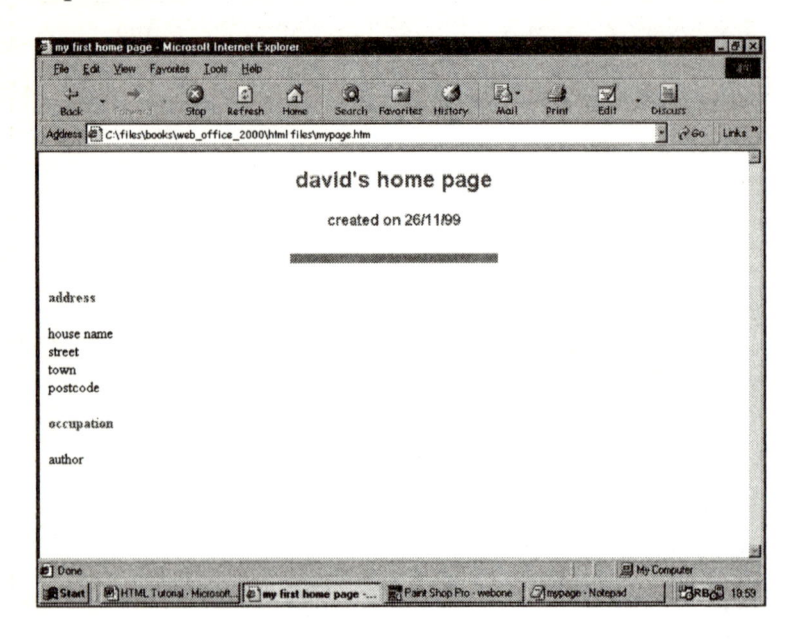

Note that the title does not appear in the page but is displayed in the title bar of the browser.

The coding for my page is as follows

```html
<html><head><title>my first home page</title></head>
<body>
<font face=arial color=e2380>
<h2 align=center>
david's home page</h2>
<h4 align=center>
created on 26/11/99</h4>
</font></font>
<hr size=10 noshade width=30%>
<h4><font color=e2380>
address
</h4></font>
house name<br>
street<br>
town<br>
postcode
<p>
<h4><font color=e2380>
occupation
</h4></font>
author
</body></html>
```

Background colours

You have already looked at the coding for text colours; it is just as easy to alter the background.

<body background="file">
This uses a picture as the background. The file is best stored in the same directory as the page.

<body bgcolor="nnnnnn">
Enter the hex value to alter the background colour.

<body text="nnnnnn">
Again this is a hex code and alters the body text colour.

You use the **body text** tag for the majority of the text and then **<font color=>** to alter text colour within the page. When you close the **</font>**, the colour of the text will revert back to the <**body text**> setting.

Exercise five

Open the file **mypage.htm** and alter the body text colour to a kind of green (hex: 21ca2), and the background to light yellow (hex: f2f4c6).

Note how the headings remain in red as you used the **font color** tag to set them, which overwrites the <**body text**> tag.

Adding graphics to your pages

You can include any graphic you wish, a company logo or a scanned picture of you and your family or employees.

The code for adding a graphic is:
<img src="image.gif">

Graphics have to be in certain file formats, i.e. .GIF or .JPG. You may have to convert your graphics file to one of these formats using a program such as **Paint Shop Pro**.

You have some control over the position of the graphics on your pages (although probably the best way to control the use of text and graphics on a page is to use tables).

The following tags **align the text to the image** (not to the page as in <**p align=center**>).

align=top (or bottom or middle)

This code is included within the IMG tag, i.e.
<img src="image.gif" align=middle>

The effect of the tag will depend upon whether the text is before or after the image in your coding.

There are many sites on the Internet offering images (including animated gifs), mostly free.

Using the Alt tag

You should include the <alt> tag to display text instead of a picture for those who have turned off the graphics or who are using older browsers.

<img src="image.gif" alt="the picture shows an image of a cat">

Space and borders

The following tags define (in pixels) the size of the image on your page, the white space around the image and put an (invisible) border (size in pixels) around the image.

> White space means space between the graphic and the text or margin, it is not necessarily white.

The number of pixels on the screen is determined by the resolution of your screen, thus if you are using 800*600 resolution, this is the number of pixels on the screen.

width=nn height=nn (can also be a % of screen)
hspace=nn vspace=nn

An example:
<img src="image.gif" width=200 height=300>

Exercise six

Find an image you like and (if necessary) convert it into **gif** format, saving it into the same folder as your web pages.

Add this to your own home page **mypage.htm,** adding the code to the line beneath the first heading on your page (Your name home page) and format it as follows:

- Size the image width and height 80 pixels.
- Put 5 pixels of white space above and below the image.
- Now align the image to the centre (you will need to use the <**p align=center**> to achieve this.

Here is an example of the additional coding:

```
<h2 align=center>
david's home page</h2>
<p align=center>
<img src=weale.gif width=80 height=80 vspace=20 >
```

Once you have the general idea, it is time to experiment, save each of these changes and view them in the browser before proceeding to the next.

- Now alter the white space to 40 pixels and again the effect changes.
- Alter the vertical white space measurement to zero and yet again look at the changes.
- Alter the horizontal rule size to 3.

At this point, your page should resemble that shown below.

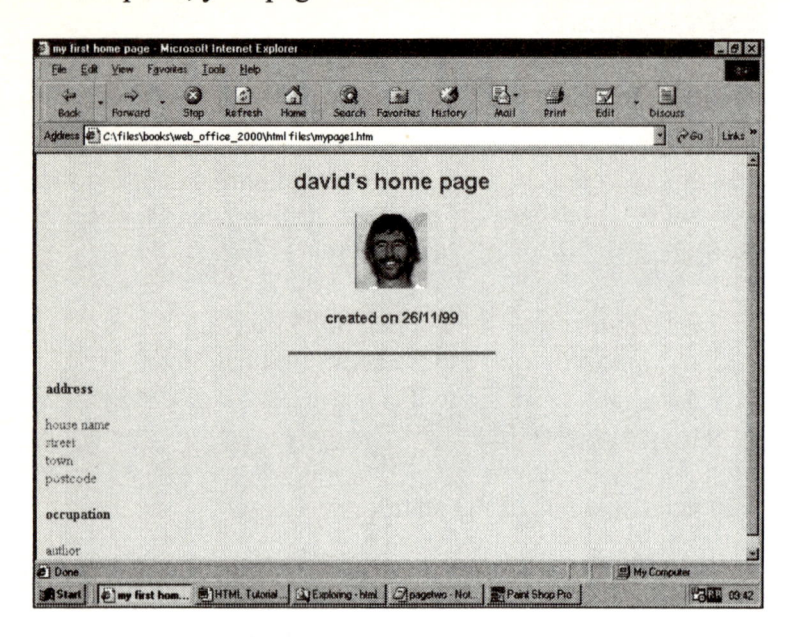

Exercise seven

Using the same file, move the line of code (for the image) above the first heading and align the image to the right.

Align all the rest of the text to the left (including the horizontal line).

Your page should now look like this.

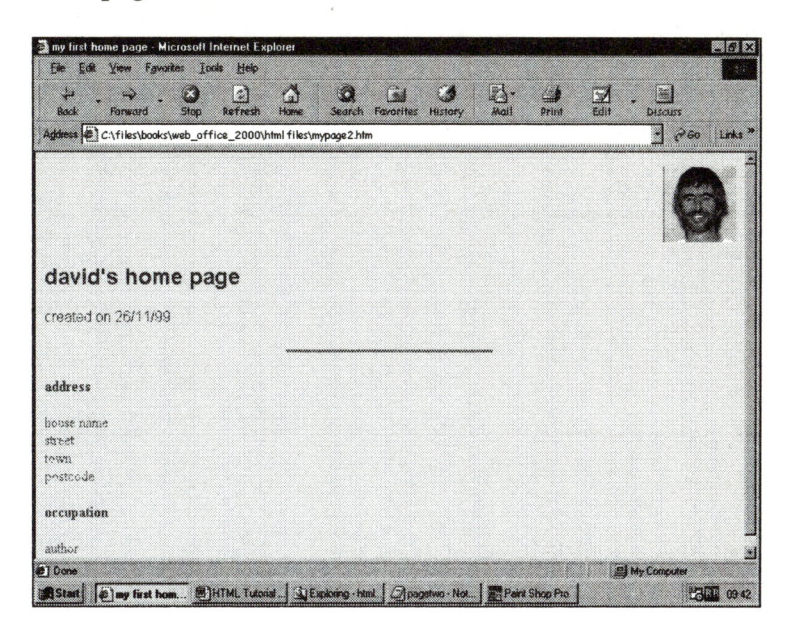

Exercise eight

The next step is to produce another page, called **pagetwo.htm**

This should contain details of the business address, telephone, a synopsis of its business activities and a contact name.

Lay this out as you wish; using the tags that have been covered so far (you do **not** need to use all of them).

My page is shown below, with the coding on the next page.

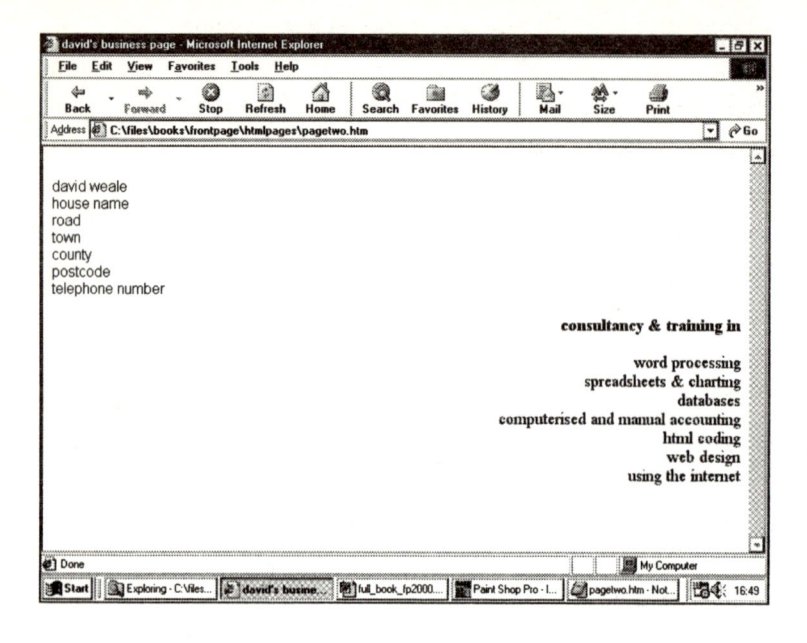

david weale
house name
road
town
county
postcode
telephone number

consultancy & training in

word processing
spreadsheets & charting
databases
computerised and manual accounting
html coding
web design
using the internet

```html
<html>
<head> <title>david's business page </title> </head>
<body>
<basefont size=4>
<pre><font face=arial>
david weale
house name
road
town
county
postcode
telephone number
</pre></font>
<font face=times new roman>
<h3 align=right>consultancy & training in</h3>
<p align=right>
word processing<br>
spreadsheets & charting<br>
databases<br>
computerised and manual accounting<br>
html coding<br>
web design<br>
using the internet<br>
</font>
</body>
</html>
```

Linking pages

You can create text and/or graphics links to other pages (these links can be to another of your pages or to pages on another site).

Text links

The coding for these is:

<a href="url">text explaining the link**</a>**

The **a** stands for an anchor and is an integral part of the syntax. The **url** is the address of the file you are linking to (whether on your hard disc or on the Internet).

> Please remember to include the text, otherwise you will have a link but nothing will appear on the page.

E-mail links

If you want the reader to email you, you have to use a special hypertext link:

<a href=mailto:your_email_address>anytext</a>

Exercise nine

Now to link your two pages together, start with **mypage.htm** and place the text link at the bottom of the page.

The URL will be the address of your second file **pagetwo.htm**

An example of the code is shown below (I have added the break tags to create space before the link).

```
<br><br>
<a href=pagetwo.htm>goto the second page</a>
```

Then open **pagetwo.htm** and insert a text link at the bottom of that page back to the first file.

When you browse either of these files (after saving the changes), you can click the link and go directly to the other page. If this happens you have been successful.

Adding email links

Add an email link to **pagetwo.htm** (make up an email address if necessary e.g. davew@someisp.co.uk). An example of the code:

```
<a href=mailto:davew@someisp.co.uk>email me</a>
```

Your page may look like this (I have place the links at the bottom of the page). If you click the email link (when you view the page in your browser), your email program should be automatically loaded so that you can send a message.

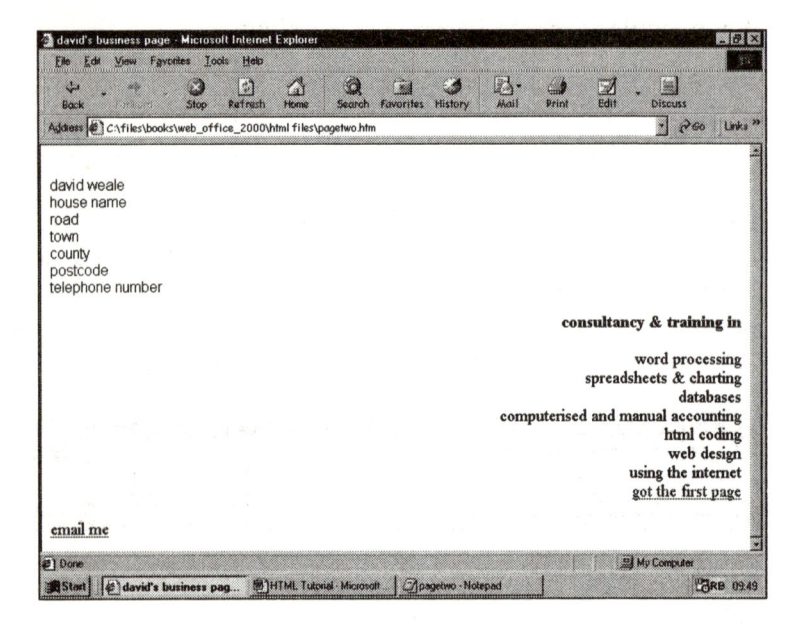

Graphics links

To use graphics as a link simply include the graphic within the hypertext code, i.e.

<a href="mypage.htm"> **<img src="arrow.gif">** click here or on the arrow to move to the previous page **</a>**

Exercise ten

Add a graphic link to your file **pagetwo.htm** (at the bottom) replacing the original text link.

An example of the coding is shown below:

```
<a href=mypage.htm><img src=arrow.gif height=30 width=100 align=left></a>
```

You will need a graphic called **arrow.gif**. You can draw one in Microsoft Paint or any graphics program if you do not have a ready-made one.

Below is an example of how the second page could look.

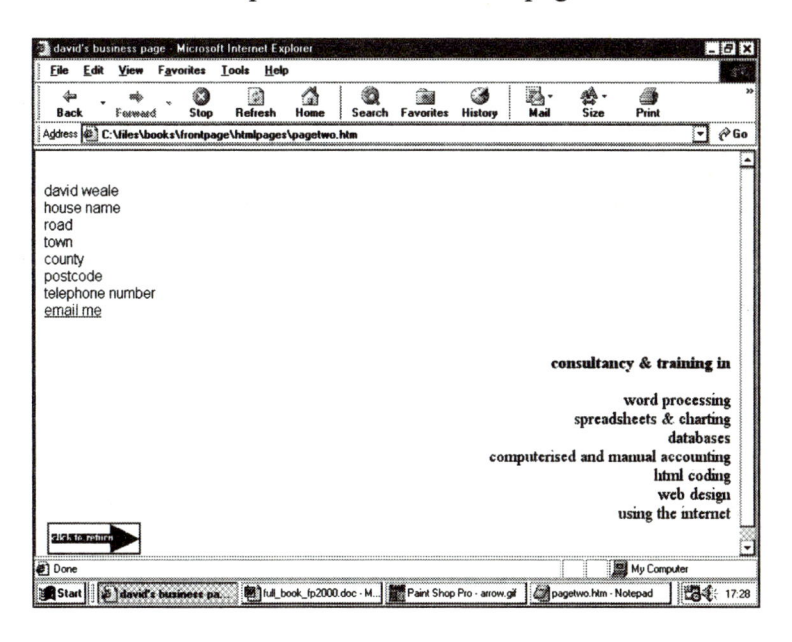

Lists

You may want to create lists of items, for example for a menu.

Unordered lists

Unordered lists display bullets on each line of the list.

The code for these is:

\<ul\>
\<li\>
\</ul\>

the **\<li\>** tag must appear before every item in the list.

If you want to introduce different style of bullets use
\<ul type="square" or "disc" or "circle"\>
which will produce square or disc bullets instead of round ones (though not necessarily in all browsers).

Ordered lists

Ordered lists are numbered lists
\<ol\>
\<li\>
\</ol\>

Nested lists

You can have lists within lists if you so wish (both numbered and bulleted lists).

```
<ul type="circle">
<li>this is a list of music I like
<li>billie holiday
<li>t-bone walker
<li>big joe turner
<li>jimmy rushing
<ul>
<li>a nested list begins here of other musicians
<li>louis jordan
<li>etta james
<li>ray charles
</ul>
</ul>
```

To begin a nested list simply start with another <ul> or <ol> **without** closing the original list.

Be careful to close the list with the closing tag </ul> or </ol> and enter this tag as many times as there are nests.

There are various changes you can make to numbered (ordered) lists.

Changing the numbering of ordered lists

<ol start=n>
Changes the start number for the list.

<li value=n>
Alters the number from that line.

<ol type=i>
Produces numeral type numbers. Also I, a, A can be used.

Using lists for links

You can create a list for your links if you want.

<ol>
<li><a href="http://www.yeovil-college.ac.uk>visit Yeovil college **</a>**
</ol>

Exercise eleven

Create a file containing **both** an unordered (bulleted) list and an ordered (numbered) list. Ensure that you have included nested lists for both.

The content of the lists can be anything you wish (if you have no ideas, perhaps you could produce a list similar to mine). Call the file **lists.htm**

Below is an example of lists.

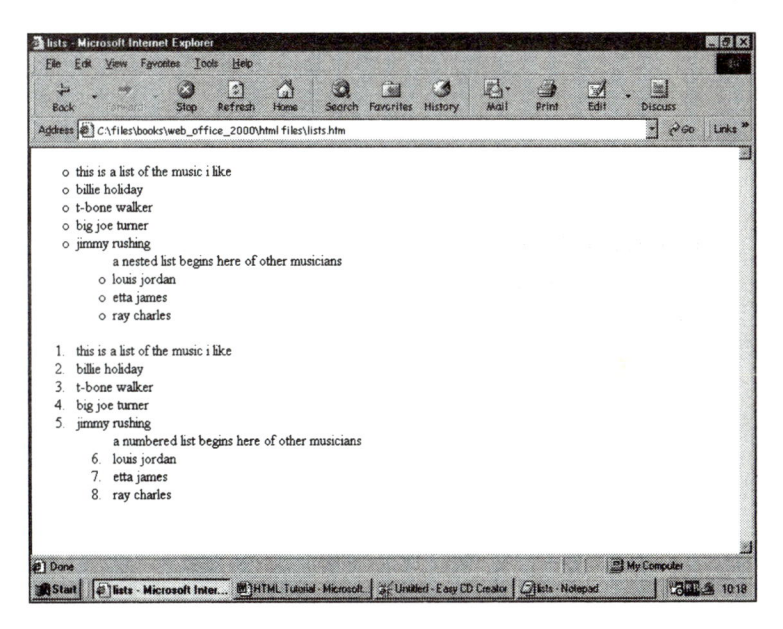

```html
<html> <head> <title>lists</title></head>
<body>
<ul type="circle">
<li>this is a list of the music i like
<li>billie holiday
<li>t-bone walker
<li>big joe turner
<li>jimmy rushing
<ul>
a nested list begins here of other musicians
<li>louis jordan
<li>etta james
<li>ray charles
</ul> </ul> <ol>
<li>this is a list of the music i like
<li>billie holiday
<li>t-bone walker
<li>big joe turner
<li>jimmy rushing
<ol>
a numbered list begins here of other musicians
<li value=6>louis jordan
<li>etta james
<li>ray charles
</ol> </ol>
</body> </html>
```

Tables

You can include text and/or graphics in the tables.

The tags

<table> </table>
The start and end of the table.

<td> </td>
Each item (i.e. a cell) is enclosed within these tags (each of these defines the column).

<tr> </tr>
Defines a row. You begin with a row, entering the columns and data for that row, then close that row and begin on the next row and so on.

Table borders

To make your table look impressive, you can add formatting. The codes are included within the <table> tag.

border=n (pixels)
cellspacing=n
cellpadding=n

An example of the coding and the subsequent table are shown below.

```
<body>
<h4>this is a table !</h4>
<table border=15 cellspacing=15 cellpadding=5>
<tr>
<td>row one, column one of the table</td>
<td>column two</td>
<td>column three</td>
</tr>
<tr>
<td>row two, column one of the table</td>
<td>column two</td>
<td>column three</td>
</tr>
</table>
</body>
```

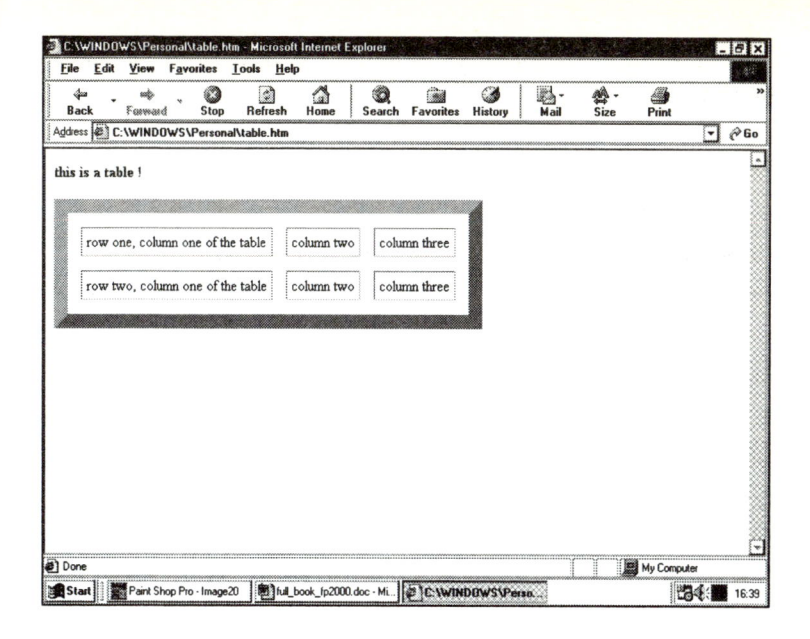

Additional table tags

Table captions

If you want to include a caption explaining the table, use the following tags.

<caption> text </caption>
You can alter the font and so on by adding the necessary code, e.g.
<caption font size=5>

Table headings

Similar to the <td> tag but the text is in bold and centred.

The tags are:
<th> </th>

Aligning text in tables

You can align text using the following additional code
align=left or **center** or **right**
valign=top or **middle** or **bottom**
(align aligns text horizontally, valign aligns vertically within the cells).

colspan=2
This merges two rows into one.

width=n
This defines the width of the column or table (in pixels or %).

Instead of text, you can include a link or a graphic.

Exercise twelve

Create a file containing a table of five rows and two columns with a caption, call the file **net.htm**. The contents of the table should be as follows:

Using the NET

Internet providers	Fixed Charge per month
Demon	Yes
Virgin Net	Yes/Variable
AOL	Variable
CompuServe	Variable

Format the table in various ways until you are happy with the result.

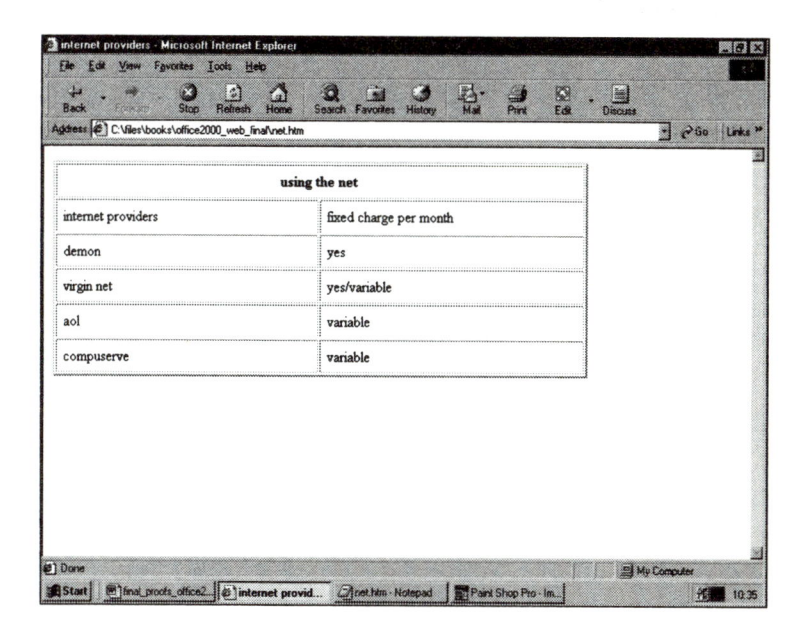

```html
<html><head><title>internet providers</title></head>
<body>
<table border=2 cellspacing=2 cellpadding=7 width=590>
<tr><td valign="middle" colspan=2>
<b><p align="center">using the net</b></td></tr>
<tr><td width="50%" valign="top">
<p>internet providers</td>
<td width="50%" valign="top">
<p>fixed charge per month</td></tr>
<tr><td width="50%" valign="top">
<p>demon</td>
<td width="50%" valign="top">
<p>yes</td></tr>
<tr><td width="50%" valign="top">
<p>virgin net</td>
<td width="50%" valign="top">
<p>yes/variable</td></tr>
<tr><td width="50%" valign="top">
<p>aol</td>
<td width="50%" valign="top">
<p>variable</td></tr>
<tr><td width="50%" valign="top">
<p>compuserve</td>
<td width="50%" valign="top">
<p>variable</td></tr>
</table></body></html>
```

Creating forms (using html)

The simplest form that you can create is a **mailto** form, the responses will be sent to you by email.

The response will come in a form that you may need to decode (by creating a macro or by using software, which is available on the Net, e.g. **www.shareware.com**).

You can format your text and page as you wish, quite often tables are used to lay out the form,

The **form** tags appear within the **body** section of the file.

It is best to keep the form as simple as possible (people generally dislike filling in forms, on-line or not).

All forms need an action type e.g.

<**Form Action**=mailto:name@isp.co.uk **Method=Post**>

This is followed by the various data entry fields and labels, you can use single line fields, scrolling text boxes, give options to select from and so on. Forms must include a **Submit** button so that the data is sent to you.

Finally you finish off the form by using the tag

</Form>

Contact us

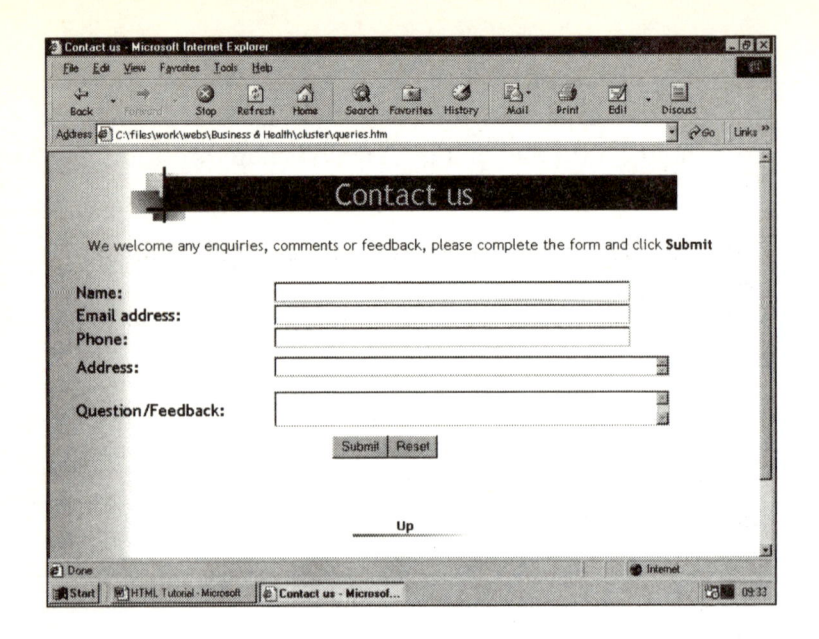

We welcome any enquiries, comments or feedback, please complete the form and click **Submit**

Name:
Email address:
Phone:

Address:

Question/Feedback:

Submit | Reset

Up

Radio buttons

Here the person completing the form selects one button from a choice.

Create a file (calling it **form.htm**) and add each of the examples (on the following pages) to this file in turn. This will build up a form containing different types of response boxes.

```
<html><head><title>
a simple form using radio buttons
</title></head>
<body>
<h2>welcome to our comments section</h2>
<h3>here are the questions</h3>
<form action=mailto:davew@isp.co.uk>
What did you like to eat <br>
<input type=radio name=dinner value=yes>
<input type=radio name=dinner value=no>
<br><br>
</form>
</body>
</html>
```

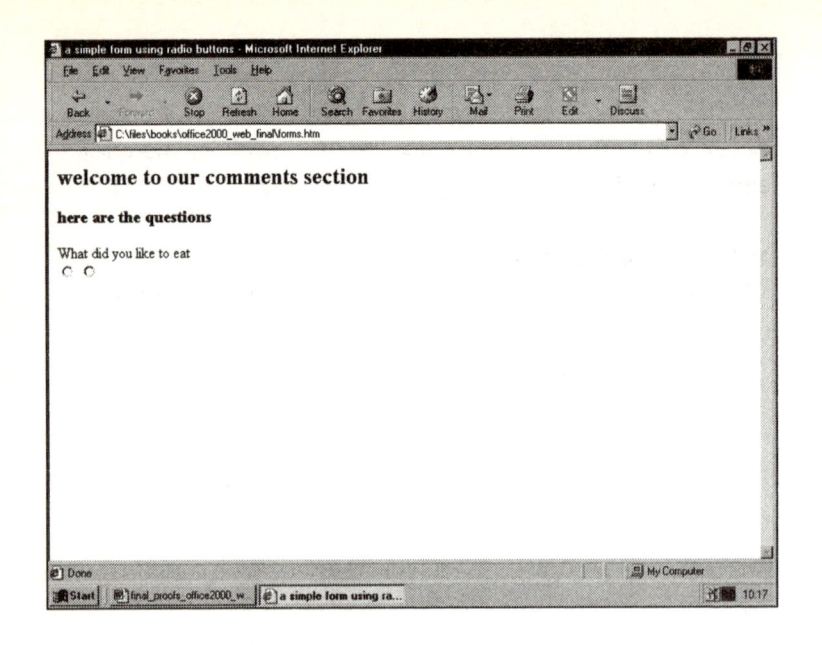

welcome to our comments section

here are the questions

What did you like to eat
○ ○

Checkboxes

These differ from radio buttons as any or all of the choices can be selected. The coding looks like this.

**What do you want to eat?
<input type=checkbox name=meat>meat dishes
<input type=checkbox name=salad>salad dishes
<input type=checkbox name=fish>fish

**

Add these lines to your form beneath the radio buttons (but before the final form tag).

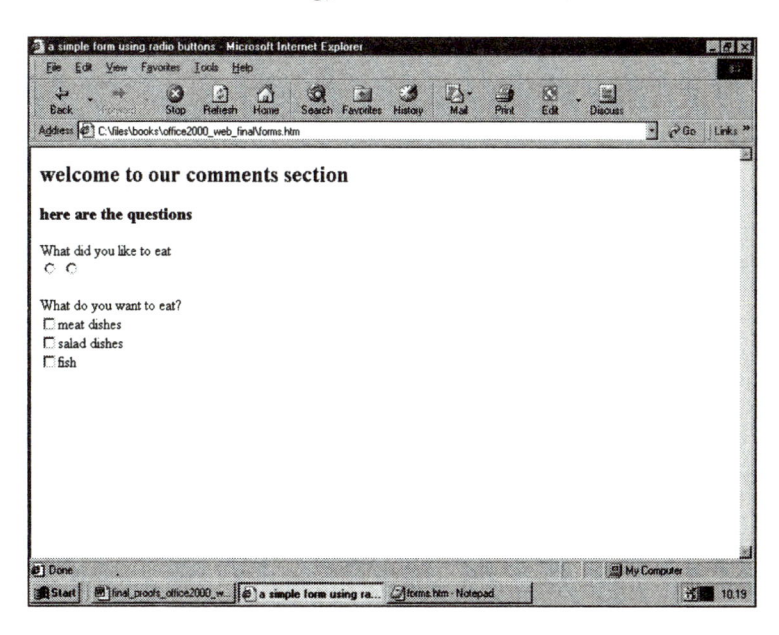

Drop-Down menus

Another way of giving choices to the reader.

What did you like to drink\<br\>
\<select name=drinks\>
\<option\>wine\<br\>
\<option\>beer\<br\>
\<option\>water\<br\>
\</select\>
\<br\>\<br\>

Add these lines to your form (after the other form tags but before the final form tag).

The illustration shows the drop-down menu after the reader has clicked the arrow to pull down the list.

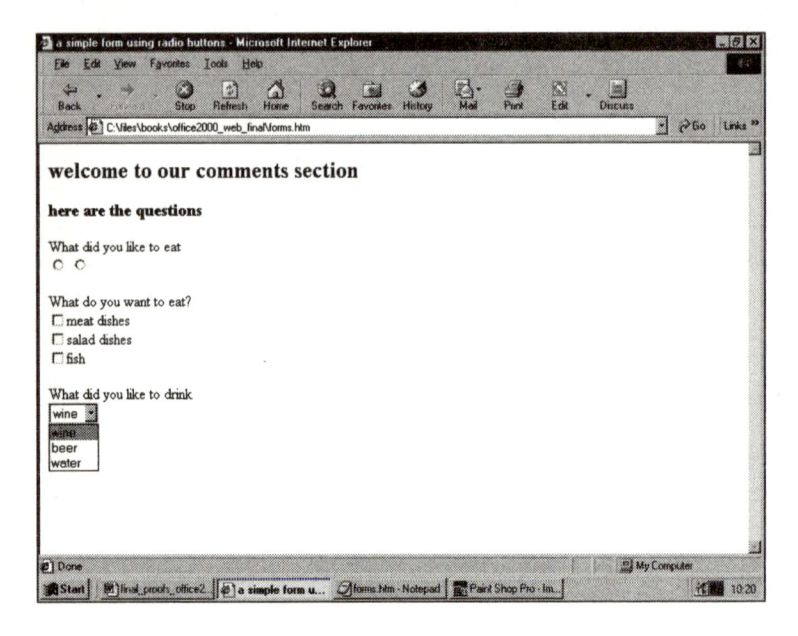

Text boxes

Often you will require your visitors to enter text, e.g. their address. You can create single-line text fields or text boxes.

please enter your telephone number
<input type=text name=phone size=40>
**

**

enter your address
<textarea name=address rows=5 cols=40>
</textarea>
**

**

Add these lines to your form (after the other form tags but before the final form tag).

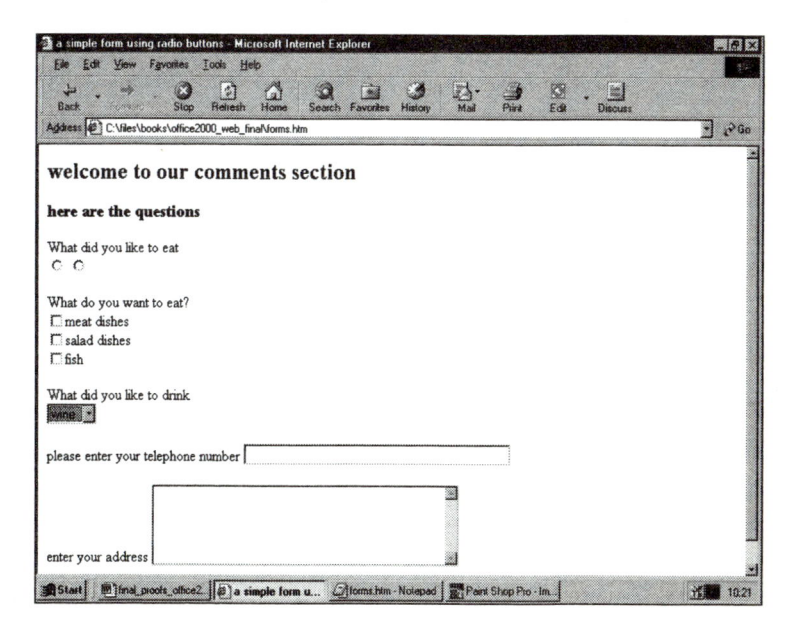

Submitting the form

Very necessary, without this your form will not be sent to you. Normally forms include both a **submit** button and a **reset** button (to clear the data). The **value** can be any text you wish.

<input type=submit value=submit>
<input type=reset value=clear>

Add these lines to your form (after the other form tags but before the final form tag). Your finished form should look something like this.

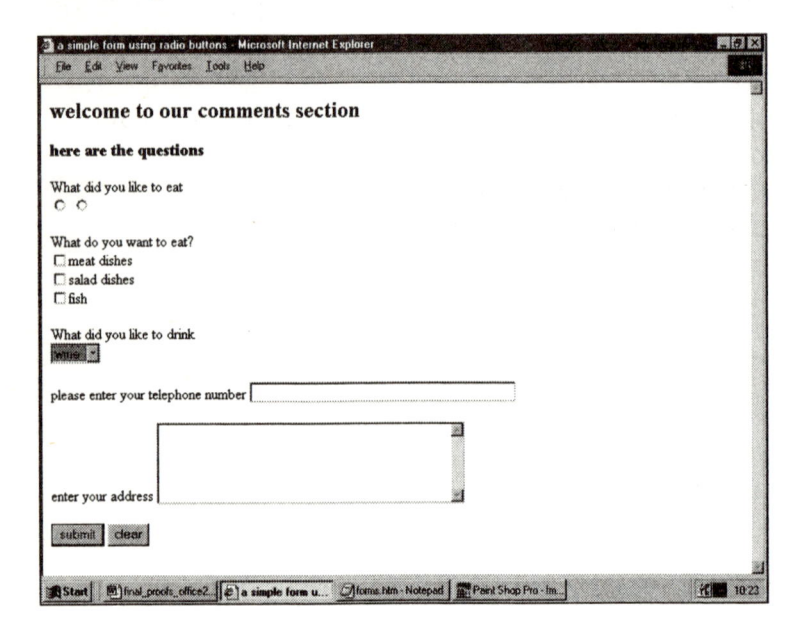

Frames

Setting up frames

This begins by setting up the frames on the page, i.e. how many columns and/or rows you want the page divided into.

<frameset rows (or **cols**) **=n,n>**
</frameset>

n is a numeric value and can be fixed (number of pixels) or % of screen or relative to remainder of windows e.g. 200,* (the * representing the remainder of space) or *,2* (this means the second value is twice the size of the first).

Next you decide what you want each frame to contain.

<frame src=contents>
The contents of each frame.

Try this exercise, saving it as **frametest.htm**

```
<html>
<head>
<title>frame exercise</title>
</head>
<frameset rows=200,*>
<frame src=mypage.htm>
<frame src=pagetwo.htm>
</frameset>
</html>
```

The result, viewed in the browser should look like this.

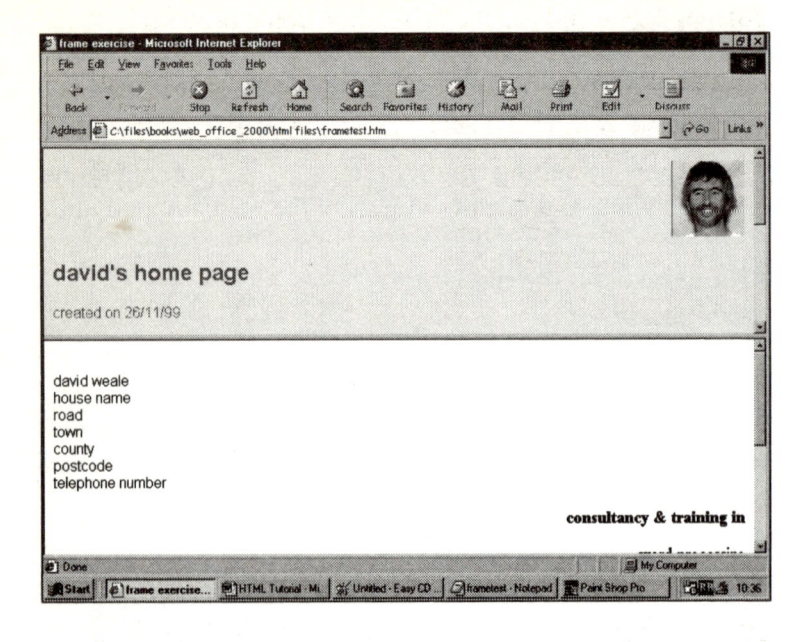

Now alter the **<frameset rows=200,*>** to **<frameset cols=40%,*>** and see the difference in the browser.

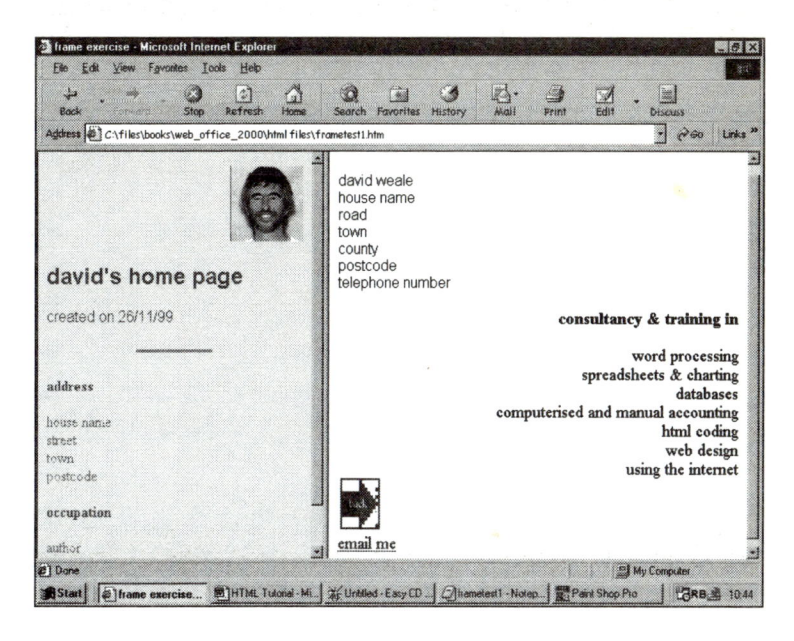

It is useful to use the **noframes** tags (directly after the **<frameset>** definition tag), e.g.

<noframes>this browser does not accept frames**</noframes>**

Browsers supporting frames ignore these tags but the message is displayed in older browsers.

Multiple frames

You can have several columns and/or rows although the more you have the greater the potential for confusion. Try this for fun, save it as **silly.htm**

```
<html>
<head>
<title>frame exercise</title>
</head>
<frameset cols=40%,*>
<frameset rows=50%,50%>
<frame src=mypage.htm>
<frame src=pagetwo.htm>
</frameset>
<frameset rows=40%,30%,30%>
<frame src=webone.htm>
<frame src=webtwo.htm>
<frame src=webthree.htm>
</frameset>
</frameset>
</html>
```

You will end up with something looking like this.

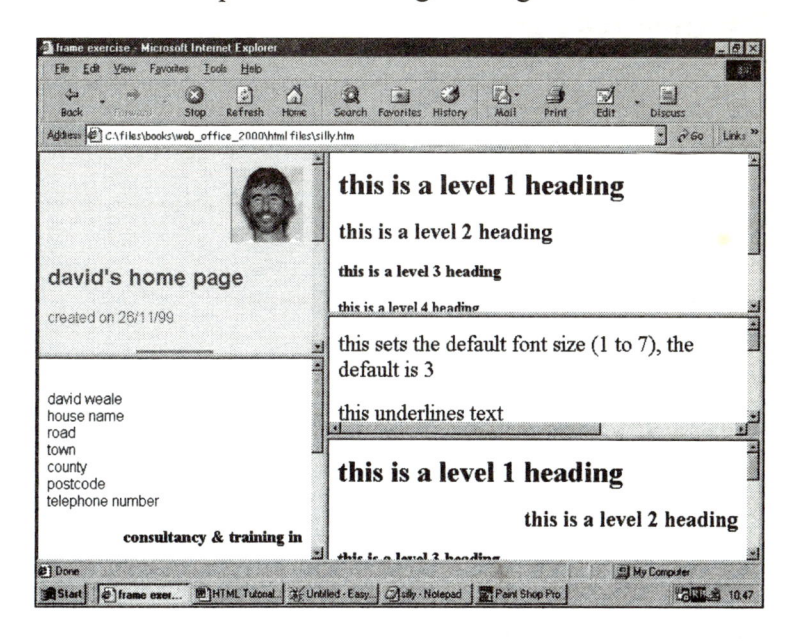

Other useful frame tags

<scrolling=yes/no/auto>
You can have scrollbars or not, or let the system decide.

<border=size in pixels>
Specifies a border around the frame

<noresize>
Prevents the user resizing the frame windows.

These tags can be combined, e.g.
<frame src=file.htm noresize scrolling=no>

Target frames

<frame src=file.htm name=name_of_frame>
If you name a frame then it can be used as a target (i.e. you can display files within that frame by calling it from another frame - see illustrated code later).

As well as an actual page, the target can be:
_self (within the same frame)
_parent (replaces the current contents with the previous)
_top (targets the whole of the window, i.e. the page is shown full screen).
_blank (a new empty window)

<a href=one.htm target=newframe>
This displays **one.htm** in the frame called **newframe**

Often frames are used to link an index page in the left frame with pages that appear in the right-hand frame as you can see in the following illustration.

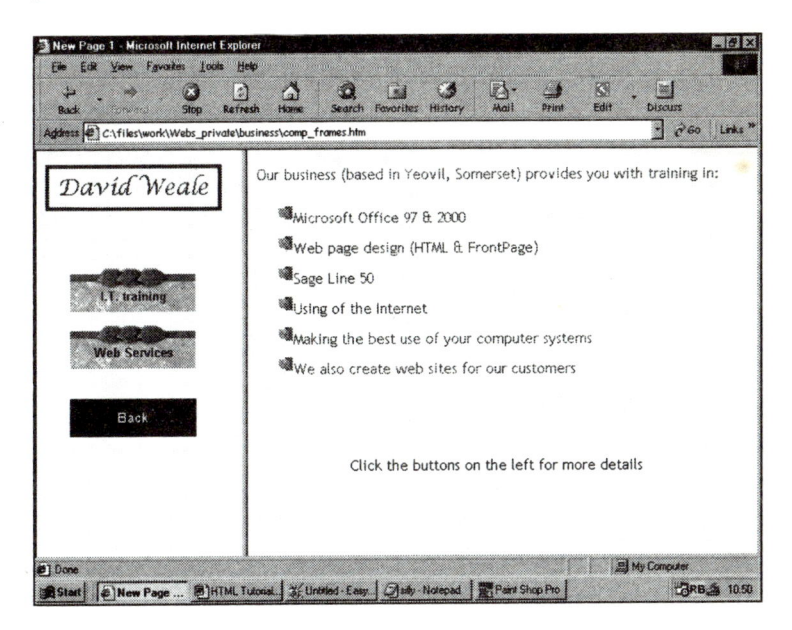

An example using linked frames

Type in these files, naming them **frames1.htm** and **frames2.htm**. The initial file that contains the structure (*the picture can be any graphic file*).

```
<html>
<frameset cols=30%,*>
<frame src=frames2.htm name=frames1>
<frame src=picture.gif name=frames2>
</frameset>
</html>
```

The following file containing the contents of the frames.

```
<html><head><title>the frame structure</title></head>
<body>
<h2>contents</h2>
<ul>
<li><a href=mypage.htm target=frames2><h4>my home page</a>
<li><a href=pagetwo.htm target=frames2>second page</h4></a>
</ul>
</body></html>
```

View the initial file (**frames1.htm**) in the browser and you should see something similar to that shown on the next page. The illustrations are of the original content page and the screen after clicking on the first item in the contents (my home page).

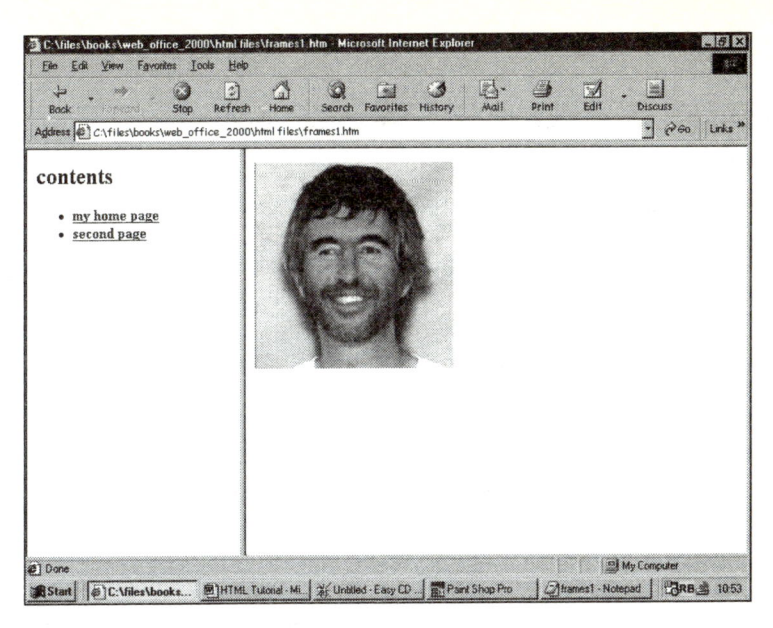

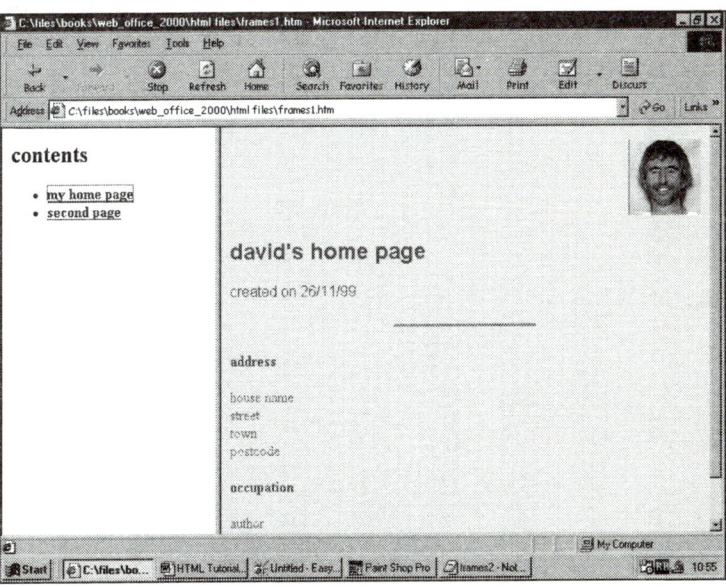

contents

- my home page
- second page

---

contents

- my home page
- second page

david's home page

created on 26/11/99

---

address

house name
street
town
postcode

occupation

author

Other Considerations

Designing web sites

First thoughts

Decide upon what you are trying to achieve and whom you are targeting.

What do you think people will want from your site?

Look at other sites, especially your competitors.

Always draw a diagram of how the site is to be structured, with an idea of what you want to include in each page and the way the pages will be linked (before beginning any coding). Planning efficiently at this stage will save hours of work later.

Try to think yourself into the same mindset as potential viewers.

Copyright

Copyright applies to web pages as much as it does to printed material (as do the laws of defamation and so on).

General design tips

Always test your pages exhaustively for sense, spelling, grammar, layout and links *and then test them again*!

Test them in both MS Explorer and Netscape, some designers create two sets of pages, each set optimised for one of the browsers.

Nowadays when the viewer may be using anything from a laptop to a 19" screen, it is worthwhile seeing how your pages look in different sized screens and at differing resolutions (there are freeware program available which let you switch between screen resolutions easily).

Try to avoid the need for the reader to scroll too much (better to start a new page using hypertext links from one to the other or use links within the page or frames).

Whether to use frames?

Think carefully before using frames; certainly avoid complex frame layouts.

On the other hand, frames are a useful way to let the user navigate around your site. Using them means that the viewer has fewer mouse clicks to arrive at any point and they can see the various choices all the time.

However recently they have fallen out of favour for the following reasons.

- They can confuse search engines.

- Only part of the screen is used for the actual content.

- Some (older) browsers find it difficult to print or save frame pages.

Backgrounds & fonts

Be very careful if you want to use textured or coloured backgrounds to your pages, they can make the text more difficult to read.

Similarly avoid irritating sounds.

Keep the design simple and do not use more than two or three fonts or colours on any page.

Links

Links should contain a description explaining why the viewer may want to look at them, and if you are using graphic links then these need to be self-explanatory.

Use standard colours for links, otherwise it can be confusing for the reader.

Make it obvious what text and pictures are links so that the reader is clear where to click the mouse.

Always and **regularly** check the links you have created (both internal and external), nothing is more irritating than broken links.

Text

Black text on a white background is traditional (after all this is how books have been produced for centuries), if you feel this is too boring then try dark colours on a light background and so on.

Blinking text (or pages) is bad news and scrolling text (marquees) and animations can become tiresome quickly and may not display properly in all browsers or screens.

Experiment, but always test new ideas with a sample of your intended audience. Some users may have larger (or smaller) monitors, consider this when choosing the smallest font size you intend to use.

Minimising file size and increasing speed

You need to experiment to get the best balance between image file size (and consequent download time) and quality of image.

You can alter the resolution, number of colours or file type for graphics in order to get the best compromise from the file format; there is a trade-off between image quality and size.

If you are using graphics that are likely to load slowly, you may want to include a **low-resolution** graphic as well; the low-resolution picture is loaded first and displays while the better quality image is loading.

Never assume that your readers are using a visual browser (even if they have a state of the art browser they may have turned off the images for speed). Always use an <**img alt**="text"> so that the reader knows what they are missing.

Remember that large files take time to download and the viewer can get irritated quickly (especially if they are paying the telephone bills). Try to avoid long download times as the viewer may click the **STOP** button.

It is recommended that the initial page should download quickly (less than 10-15 seconds at average download speeds).

Site Structure

Divide your site into a series of pages, each with a link to the next and previous, and organise them in a coherent and logical way.

Each page should contain links to your home page, as the user may have jumped to a page on your site that is not your home page.

> There is a concept called the **3-click rule**, this says that no page should be more than three mouse clicks away.

You should also try to avoid confusing the reader by giving them too many buttons to click on any one page (possibly six is a good maximum).

Reverse engineering

Spend some time looking around the Net at the way in which pages and sites are constructed. You will learn much.

I suggest you look at the source code of the pages you find attractive. There is nothing wrong with adapting other people's ideas; this is very different from plagiarism.

Getting readers for your site

Include your URL in all company literature (letters, invoices, advertising, etc.).

Maintain the site by checking the contents regularly and update the information **and links** (out-of-date information is a quick way to kill interest in a site).

To make your site interesting, add new material regularly.

Use forms and/or counters to analyse the response to the site.

Include your E-mail address and if you are expecting a response from abroad remember to include your international dialling code for telephone or fax replies.

Will your pages be found?

Get your site included in as many search engines as possible, as long as they are relevant and are likely to be used by your potential viewers.

In practice this means the major engines plus any minor engines that deal with your type of subject matter and/or geographic region.

It is preferable to submit your site yourself to the major engines, rather than rely on the automated submission services.

Normally the search engines will follow the links to the remainder of your pages, indexing as they go.

There will be a time delay between submitting your URL and your pages being indexed, this can be several weeks so be patient.

It is worthwhile re-registering whenever you make major changes to your site, as it may be some time before the engines revisit your site.

What search engines index

Search engines do not always index the same type of material, e.g. some index the contents of **Meta** tags.

Engines often list the page title in search results so it is important to have a title that is understandable and clearly explains the purpose of your page.

Keywords

Most search engines rank your pages based upon the placement and frequency of keywords. Including keywords in the following places should increase your ranking.

TITLE tag

Keyword & Description Meta tags

First 25 words of body text

In <! Comments tags

Inside <ALT> tags

Inside NO FRAMES tags

You are more likely to get a high listing if your keywords are two (or more) words long. This is simply because single words are more likely to occur in pages and your pages are therefore competing with many other pages.

Where you position the keywords is of importance. It is vital that the **title** tag includes your primary keywords as most search engines use this.

Try to use keywords in headings and as high up the page as possible, as search engines will give them more importance.

Look at the source code for highly ranked sites, seeing how they use keywords to obtain a high ranking.

While tables are a useful layout technique, they can make keywords included within them appear of less relevance (simply because of the way in which search engines read tables).

Some search engines will not read image maps or links contained within frames.

Meta tags

The **description** Meta tag appears in place of the summary which the search engine would normally print in the search results.

The **keyword** Meta tag should include any keywords you want the search engine to associate with your page. The keyword Meta tag provides keywords to match with the words the viewer types in when using the search engine.

When creating the keyword **Meta tag**, think about the kind of keywords you would use if you were searching for information similar to that contained within your pages.

An example of how to use Meta tags is shown below.

```html
<html><head>
<meta name="description" content="computer training & problem solving">
<meta name="keywords" content="lecturer, writing web pages, computer advice">
<title>david weale's business page
</title>
</head>
<body>make sure you include keywords within the content of your page, although this is unlikely to be a problem
</body></html>
```

Search engines that make use of Meta tags will display the following descriptions when displaying the results of a search, the first line from the title tag and the second from the description Meta tag.

```
david weale's business page
computer training & problem solving
```

How you access the Net

Buy a computer and modem and sign up with an ISP (Internet Service Provider).

Internet Service Providers

Pay-for services

AOL, CompuServe, Demon, UUNet Pipex, these charge (normally a fixed monthly charge) and offer certain facilities unavailable to non-subscribers, e.g. specialist forums or content.

There are many Internet Service Providers who provide a service specifically for business users. They may provide domain names and other services which businesses require, for example secure servers for e-commerce purposes.

Free services

Examples of these include Freeserve, Virgin and Screaming Net. There are no monthly charges but you may have on-screen advertising and slow response times. They are not specifically business orientated.

Some of these are offering free telephone charges for Internet access, but normally expect you to change your telecom provider to one of their choice.

Choosing a provider

- What services do you actually want?

- How are the charges calculated?

- How much web space for your own site?

- How many email addresses are provided?

- Can the IP handle on-line forms?

- Do you require e-commerce facilities?

Connections

Dial-up

A standard telephone connection, this is relatively slow and you need an additional line if you need to make phone calls while you are connected to the Internet.

ISDN

If you intend to use your connection regularly investigate the use of an ISDN line, set-up costs are comparable with a second telephone line but running costs differ. Offers 64 KBPS speed and is generally faster and more reliable. They do not use standard modems but need a special ISDN box, which costs roughly the same as a good modem.

Leased lines

Sometimes called kilostream lines. These are expensive and may be viable for certain users or if you want to run your own web site. They are permanent connections and a yearly payment covers all costs, however long you are connected.

Domains

A domain is a unique address, which appears after the letters WWW in a Net address

http://www.yeovil-college.ac.uk
The domain is yeovil-college (ac stands for academic and uk for the united kingdom)

Why have a domain

For an organisation, it makes sense to have its own domain; it is your address or telephone number on the Net. Your organisation is therefore much easier to locate, it strengthens your competitive position and builds brand awareness.

Getting a domain name

You need to obtain a domain name and register it with a Network Information Centre (NIC). The UK one is called NOMINET (the site contains much useful information on domain names).
http://www.nic.uk/

You can transfer it to another ISP, and once registered you have to pay annual administration fees and rental.

Hosting your web site

Using an ISP to host your site
This makes use of a virtual server, the ISP is hosting you but the ISP name does not appear in your Net address (assuming your have your own domain).

You are buying space on the host server; you pay a set-up fee and a rental for this, however as far as the public is concerned you have your own server.

Using your own server
You set up your own server and connect to the Internet infrastructure (the backbone).

You can connect to the Internet via one of the companies offering connection to the backbone, e.g. BTnet, U-Net.

Your server needs to be on-line 24 hours a day and you need a leased line connection, as a modem is not really sufficient.

Glossary

Archie	A program to find on-line material - an older form of retrieval, superseded by the WWW
Backbone	The infrastructure of the internet, data travels from one network to another via the backbone
Bandwidth	How much data can be sent along a connection
Baud rate	Measures the speed of data travelling along communication lines, measured in KBPS (kilobytes per second)
Browser	The program that enables you to view HTML documents (both on-line and off-line)
Dial-up	Connect to the Net
Domain	The address of the host computer
Download	Transfer data from a web site to your computer
E-mail	Electronic mail - you have an e-mail address in a similar way to your home address
FAQ	Frequently asked question, many sites have a list of FAQs so you can learn the basics about the site
Flame	An e-mail (not nice) sent to the originator of a message, it has been known for thousands of people to flame a particular site, jamming the server
FTP	File Transfer Protocol - a quick way of transferring files from one Net site to another

Gopher	Means 'Go For' - a method of finding the information you require using a menu system - the antecedent of the WWW
Home page	The first page for a site (normally Index.htm)
HTML	Hypertext mark-up language - the code in which web pages are written
HTTP	Hypertext transfer protocol (how HTML documents get transferred around the Net)
Hypertext link	A link from one web page to another, it can be text or a graphic
Intranet	An internal (company) internet using the same protocols, it makes accessing company-wide data easy and cheap compared with traditional methods (only one copy of documents exist and they are held centrally on the server)
JavaScript	A programming language for internet applications
Modem	Modulator/demodulator - hardware that translates digital data into analogue and back again (so the data can travel the telephone system)
Netiquettc	Behave or you will be flamed
Newsgroup	A Usenet discussion group
On-line	Connected to the Net and using the telephone lines, off-line means using Net tools, e.g. browsers without being connected
POP	Point of presence
Plug-ins	Additional programs for web browsers
Server	The computer which hosts the web site

Snail mail	Traditional physical post systems
Spam	Sending a message to many Usenet newsgroups - normally a breach of Netiquette (you may get flamed as a result)
Telnet	Allows you to take control of a remote computer - obviously access is restricted to certain public sites
URL	Uniform Resource Locator - the address
Winsock	A Windows file that enables Windows to communicate with the Net servers
WWW	World Wide Web

Index

3-Click Rule 162

A

Access 72, 92, 93
Action Buttons 87
Animation 89
Autofit 48

B

Backbone 172, 174
Background 114
Bandwidth 174
Baud rate 174
Bookmark 35
Borders 116, 131
Bullets 28, 126

C

Caption 133, 135
Catalog 54, 55
Change Case 43
Checkboxes 141
Convert 49, 115, 117
Copyright 156
Counters 163
Custom Animation 89

D

Design Checker	79
Design Gallery	75
Dial-up	170, 174
Domain	168, 171, 172, 174
Download	30, 36, 80, 161, 174
Drop Cap	42

E

E-Commerce	168, 169
Excel	92, 93

F

FAQ	174
Fill	28
Flame	174
Folder	12, 85, 94, 100, 117
Forms	5, 39, 59, 137, 144, 163, 169
Frames	145, 152, 157, 158, 166
FrontPage	93
FTP	94, 174

G

GIF	30, 115, 116, 117, 124, 125, 151
Gopher	175

H

Heading	99, 101, 102, 109, 111, 117, 118
Highlight	26, 27, 28, 34, 47
Home page	3, 111, 113, 117, 152, 162, 175
Hotspots	78
HTTP	128, 171, 175
Hyperlink	6, 34, 76, 77, 78, 86, 87, 88

I

Internet	82, 87
Internet Address	176
Intranet	76, 87, 175
ISDN	170
ISP	19, 59, 94, 137, 139, 168, 171, 172

J

Java	175
JPEG	30

K

Keywords	165, 166, 167
Kilostream	170

L

Line Break	99
Lists	126, 127, 128, 129, 130

M

Mailto	122, 123, 137, 139
Marquee	38
Meta tags	165, 166, 167
Modem	168, 170, 172, 175
Movie	7, 89
Multi-media	5, 7, 36, 37

N

Nested Lists	127, 129
Netiquette	175, 176
Newsgroup	175
NIC	171
Numbering	28, 128

O

On-line	5, 137, 169, 172, 174, 175
Outline	84, 92

P

Pixels	108, 111, 116, 117, 131, 134
Plug-ins	175
POP	175
Properties	50
Publish	83

R

Radio Button	139, 141
Refresh	100
Reset	32, 63, 144
Resolution	19, 103, 116, 161

S

Server	172, 174, 175
Snail mail	176
Sound	5, 7, 36, 37, 60, 65, 89
Source	24, 100, 162, 166
Spam	176
Speed	174
Spelling	103
Style	98, 99, 126
Submit	137, 144, 164
Symbol	97

T

Telnet	176
Template	13
Theme	11, 15
Toolbar	51
Troubleshooter	80

U

URL	77, 78, 122, 123, 163, 164, 176
Usenet	175, 176

V

Video	36, 37

W

Web	80, 82, 83, 85
Winsock	176
WWW	128, 171, 174, 175, 176